KV-056-300

Preface

A wide range of books offer introductions to microprocessor technology. These texts offer descriptions of the fundamental principles of microelectronic circuits and the operation and programming of microprocessors. However, they stop short of a rigorous analysis of how microcomputers can be connected to external devices and peripherals. This book examines interfacing techniques and circuits in detail. It covers the principal interfacing components and explores how these devices can be applied in circuit form and programmed to perform interfacing duties. Methods of connecting microcomputers to printers, VDUs, television monitors, displays, keyboards, electrical control equipment, other computers, plant instrumentation, and a comprehensive list of specific devices is included. Interfacing components and systems from the following manufacturers are examined in detail: Intel, Zilog, Texas Instruments, MOS Technology, BBC, Apple.

Additional material, which covers the principles of microcomputers, is included, so that the book provides a complete learning guide to the basic fundamentals of microcomputer technology as well as emphasising interfacing techniques. For example, Chapters 1, 2 and 7 describe the general technology (logic, circuit building-blocks and programming), whilst the remaining bulk of the book directs the reader through the principles and details of interfacing.

A glossary explaining the most frequently used terms can be found at the end of the book.

The author wishes to thank his family and colleagues for their support during the preparation of this book.

COMPUTERS
and their
INTERFACING

Other Pergamon titles of interest

Books

DEBENHAM	Microprocessors: Principles & Applications
DUMMER	Electronic Inventions & Discoveries, 3rd Edition
ERA	The Engineering of Microprocessor Systems
GHANDI	Microwave Engineering & Applications
GUILE & PATERSON	Electrical Power Systems, Volume 1, 2nd Edition
	Electrical Power Systems, Volume 2, 2nd Edition
HAMMOND	Electromagnetism for Engineers, 2nd Edition (in SI/Metric Units)
HINDMARSH	Electrical Machines & Their Applications, 4th Edition Worked Examples in Electrical Machines & Drives
HOLLAND	Microcomputers for Process Control
MALLER & NAIDU	Advances in High Voltage Insulation & Arc Interruption in SF_6 & Vacuum
MURPHY	Power Semiconductor Control of Motors & Drives
RODDY	Introduction to Microelectronics, 2nd Edition
SMITH	Analysis of Electrical Machines
WAIT	Wave Propagation Theory
YORKE	Electric Circuit Theory

Journals of related interest (*Free specimen copy gladly sent on request*)

Computers & Electrical Engineering
Electric Technology USSR
Microelectronics & Reliability
Solid State Electronics

MICROCOMPUTERS
and their
INTERFACING

by

R. C. HOLLAND
West Glamorgan Institute of Higher Education, UK

PERGAMON PRESS
OXFORD · NEW YORK · TORONTO · SYDNEY · PARIS · FRANKFURT

U.K.	Pergamon Press Ltd., Headington Hill Hall, Oxford OX3 0BW, England
U.S.A	Pergamon Press Inc., Maxwell House, Fairview Park, Elmsford, New York 10523, U.S.A.
CANADA	Pergamon Press Canada Ltd., Suite 104, 150 Consumers Road, Willowdale, Ontario M2J 1P9, Canada
AUSTRALIA	Pergamon Press (Aust.) Pty. Ltd., P.O. Box 544, Potts Point, N.S.W. 2011, Australia
FRANCE	Pergamon Press SARL, 24 rue des Ecoles, 75240 Paris, Cedex 05, France
FEDERAL REPUBLIC OF GERMANY	Pergamon Press GmbH, Hammerweg 6, 6242 Kronberg-Taunus, Federal Republic of Germany

Copyright © 1984 Pergamon Press Ltd.

All Rights Reserved. No part of this publication may be reproduced, stored in a retrieval system or transmitted in any form or by any means: electronic, electrostatic, magnetic tape, mechanical, photocopying, recording or otherwise, without permission in writing from the publishers.

First edition 1984

Library of Congress Cataloging in Publication Data
Holland, R. C.
Microcomputers and their interfacing.
Includes index.
1. Microcomputers. 2. Computer interfaces. I. Title.
TK7888.3.H65 1984   001.64   84–2828

British Library Cataloguing in Publication Data
Holland, R. C.
Microcomputers and their interfacing.
1. Microcomputers   2. Computers interfaces
I. Title
001.64′04   TK7888.3

ISBN 0-08-031124-5
ISBN 0-08-031125-3 Pbk

Printed in Great Britain by A. Wheaton & Co. Ltd., Exeter

621.381952

Contents

CHAPTER 1

Microcomputer Fundamentals

(It is assumed that most readers are familiar with the basic concepts of computer operation, including binary numbers, logic, voltage levels and the physical appearance of silicon chip devices. However, a short introduction is presented in this first chapter on such topics for the benefit of readers who are new to the subject of microcomputers and their interfacing circuits.)

1.1 BINARY AND HEXADECIMAL NUMBERS

Man has long used the base of 10 for his number system. Numbers in this system are called **decimal** (or denary), and a straightforward number of 285 can be elaborated as follows:

- Decimal $285 = 285_{10} = 2 \times 10^2 + 8 \times 10^1 + 5 \times 10^0$
$$= \quad 200 \quad + \quad 80 \quad + \quad 5$$

Computer circuits cannot easily handle ten different signal levels. It is far easier to design such circuits to handle just two levels, e.g. voltage and no voltage. Thus numbers are handled by computers in **binary** notation, which uses a base of 2. In this age of information technology, which is dominated by microelectronic circuits and microcomputers, man is forced to learn this second number system if he is to fully understand this new technology. For example:

$$\text{Binary } 1100 = 1100_2 = 1 \times 2^3 + 1 \times 2^2 + 0 \times 2^1 + 0 \times 2^0$$
$$= \quad 8 \quad + \quad 4 \quad + \quad 0 \quad + \quad 0$$

1

Therefore, binary 1100 = decimal 12.

Each binary digit, or "bit", can be 0 or 1. Individual bits represent increasing "powers of 2".

The method of converting binary numbers to decimal numbers is as follows:

$$1001_2 = 1 \times 2^3 + 0 \times 2^2 + 0 \times 2^1 + 1 \times 2^0$$
$$= 8 + 0 + 0 + 1$$
$$= 9_{10}.$$

There are two common methods of performing conversion in the opposite direction, as follows.

Method A—continually divide by 2

Convert 14_{10} to binary.

$$
\begin{array}{ll}
1 & 1 \leftarrow \text{remainder 3} \\
2\overline{)\,3} & 1 \leftarrow \text{remainder 2} \\
2\overline{)\,7} & 0 \leftarrow \text{remainder 1} \\
2\overline{)14} &
\end{array}
$$

Answer $= 1110_2$.

Method B—express directly in "powers of 2"

Convert 14_{10} to binary.

$$
\begin{array}{ccccccccc}
& 8(2^3) & & 4(2^2) & & 2(2^1) & & 1(2^0) & \\
\hline
14_{10} = & 1 & + & 1 & + & 1 & + & 0 & = 1110_2
\end{array}
$$

This method requires some agile mental arithmetic or the use of a scrap of paper to express the decimal number in its components, which are powers of 2 (1, 2, 4, 8, 16, 32, 64, etc.).

For example:

$$
\begin{array}{ccccccccc}
128 & 64 & 32 & 16 & 8 & 4 & 2 & 1 \\
\hline
163_{10} = \quad 1 & 0 & 1 & 0 & 0 & 0 & 1 & 1 & = 1010\ 0011_2.
\end{array}
$$

Notice that in this last example a gap is inserted between the two groups of 4 bits. This grouping of 4 bits is convention, and it helps to prevent

TABLE 1.1. NUMBER SYSTEMS

Decimal	Binary	Hexadecimal
0	0000	0
1	0001	1
2	0010	2
3	0011	3
4	0100	4
5	0101	5
6	0110	6
7	0111	7
8	1000	8
9	1001	9
10	1010	A
11	1011	B
12	1100	C
13	1101	D
14	1110	E
15	1111	F

mistakes when expressing large binary numbers. Also it means that binary numbers, which tend to be extremely long, can be expressed much more concisely if a code is used for each group of 4 bits. For example:

$$1001 \quad 0111 \quad 1000 \quad 0100 \quad \leftarrow \text{ binary number}$$
$$9 \quad\quad 7 \quad\quad 8 \quad\quad 4 \quad\quad \leftarrow \text{ "hexadecimal" code}$$

Each group of 4 bits is described as a number which can have a value between decimal 0 and 15. However, to avoid using two characters in place of one after 9 is passed, the letters A, B, C, D, E and F are applied. This leads to the use of the "hexadecimal" code, which expresses numbers in "powers of 16".

The relationships between decimal, binary and hexadecimal numbers are described in Table 1.1.

Examine the following examples:

EXAMPLE 1

Express binary $\quad 0010 \quad 1100 \quad 0110 \quad 1010 \quad$ in hexadecimal
$$2 \quad\quad C \quad\quad 6 \quad\quad A \quad\quad (= 2C6A_{16})$$

EXAMPLE 2

Express hex. 32D5 in binary (hex. = abbreviation for hexadecimal)
$$0011\ 0010\ 1101\ 0101_2$$

EXAMPLE 3

Convert $B9_{16}$ to decimal
$$B(11_{10}) \times 16^1 + 9 \times 16^0$$
$$= \quad 176 \quad + \quad 9 \quad = 185_{10}$$

EXAMPLE 4

Convert 138_{10} to hex. (firstly convert to binary, and then group into hex. codes)

	128	64	32	16	8	4	2	1
$138_{10} =$	1	0	0	0	1	0	1	0

$$= 1000\ 1010_2$$
$$= 8A_{16}.$$

Microcomputers tend to express numbers and to handle bit patterns in groups of 8 bits or 16 bits.

1.2 BINARY ARITHMETIC

Binary arithmetic is performed using the same general rules as for decimal arithmetic. Consider the following examples:

EXAMPLE 1

Add $0011\ 0100_2$ to $0111\ 0110_2$

$$\begin{array}{r} 0011\ 0100 \\ 0111\ 0110 \\ \hline 1010\ 1010 \end{array} +$$

EXAMPLE 2

Subtract $0011\ 1000_2$ from $0101\ 0101_2$

$$\begin{array}{r} 0101\ 0101 \\ 0011\ 1000 \\ \hline 0001\ 1101 \end{array}\ -$$

Multiplication and division merely extend these general rules. It must be mentioned that all lower-powered (8-bit) microcomputers cannot actually perform multiplication and division by hardware. These arithmetic functions must be performed with clever programming procedures which utilise addition and subtraction. However, all higher-powered (16-bit) machines offer these functions.

Negative numbers are held within microcomputers using the "twos complement" notation. In this method the left-hand (or most significant) bit of the number represents the sign, viz. 0 = positive, 1 = negative. If this bit is 1, then the other bits represent the magnitude of the negative number in twos complement form, as follows:

$$\text{sign bit} \rightarrow \underbrace{1111\ 0111}$$

$$\downarrow \text{ invert all bits}$$
$$0000\ 1000$$
$$\downarrow \text{ add 1}$$
$$\text{magnitude of} \rightarrow 0000\ 1001$$
$$\text{negative number}$$

Therefore, the number is -9_{10}.

The same rules of conversion (invert all bits, add 1) apply in the opposite direction, i.e. to generate a twos complement number, e.g.

$$+12_{10} = 0000\ 1100$$

invert all bits: $1111\ 0011$

add 1: $1111\ 0100$

Therefore, $-12_{10} = 1111\ 0100_2$.

A rather distinctive twos complement number, which experienced computer programmers encounter frequently, is all 1s:

$1111\ 1111_2$ which equals -1_{10}

The reader may like to check this relationship using the rules described above.

1.3 LOGIC

Many signals, which are external to a computer, are "analogue" or continuous in form, e.g. a room temperature reading. Naturally such signals must be converted to a digital form, in fact to a binary digital form using 1s and 0s only, before processing can occur within a computer. Additionally, "logical" functions are often performed on bits which represent external events or readings, as well as on other signals. Such logic functions can be performed by "hardware" (electronic circuitry) or "software" (computer program).

The main logic functions are:

(a) AND

Two single-bit signals can be "gated" together to produce a composite AND signal output as shown in Fig. 1.1. The "truth table" is also shown; this illustrates the effect of all different combinations of signals.

The operation of the AND gate can be seen, therefore, to produce a 1 output only if both inputs are at 1.

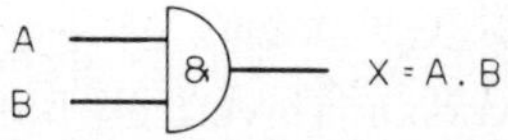

A ———⊐&⊃——— X = A . B
B ———

(a) Circuit symbol

A	B	X = A.B
0	0	0
0	1	0
1	0	0
1	1	1

(b) Truth table

FIG. 1.1. AND gate.

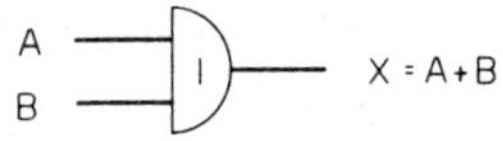

(a) Circuit symbol

A	B	X = A + B
0	0	0
0	1	1
1	0	1
1	1	1

(b) Truth table

FIG. 1.2. OR gate.

(b) OR

Figure 1.2 shows the circuit symbol and truth table for an OR gate. This produces a 1 output if either or both of its inputs are at 1.

(c) Inverter (or Complementer)

Figure 1.3 shows the action of an inverter, i.e. a gate which inverts, or complements, a single-bit signal from 0 to 1 and from 1 to 0. The bar above the signal identity denotes inversion. Alternative circuits are shown to perform the same function; this may be helpful in some microelectronic systems to avoid a proliferation of gate types. Notice that the gate types which are used are NAND and NOR gates, i.e. they invert (shown by the circle at the output connection) as well as perform the AND and OR logic functions. In practice it is found that circuit elements can be made far more easily if inversion is included. The truth tables for the NAND and NOR functions are shown in Fig. 1.4.

Gates of these types are sometimes required when handling external signals to microcomputers, and occasionally also within certain parts of the overall microcomputer circuit. In this case the signals 0 and 1 are normally represented by voltage levels of 0 V and +5 V respectively. More importantly the central processing unit (called CPU or "microprocessor") part of the microcomputer can perform these operations on

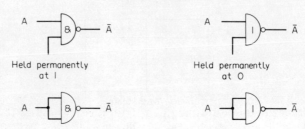

(a) Circuit symbol

(b) Four different circuit alternatives

A	$\bar{A}$
0	1
1	0

(c) Truth table

FIG. 1.3. Inverter (complementer).

multi-bit numbers or bit patterns. For example, an 8-bit machine performs an AND operation on two 8-bit values as follows:

$$A = 0101 \ 1001$$
$$B = 0000 \ 1111$$
$$A \cdot B = \overline{0000 \ 1001}$$

The AND operation is performed separately on the corresponding bit in each data value. The action in this case can be seen to "mask out" the top 4 bits, i.e. set these bits to 0, in the results of $A \cdot B$.

The action of the OR operation can be seen to introduce 1s, as follows:

$$A = 0010 \ 0111$$
$$B = 1111 \ 0000$$
$$A + B = \overline{1111 \ 0111}$$

A	B	A̅.̅B̅
0	0	1
0	1	1
1	0	1
1	1	0

A	B	A̅+̅B̅
0	0	1
0	1	0
1	0	0
1	1	0

(a) NAND gate   (b) NOR gate

Fig. 1.4. Truth tables for NAND and NOR gates.

The microprocessor stores these multi-bit data values in "registers" whilst it is processing them. For example, a 16-bit register holds a 16-bit data value. The microprocessor possesses only a small number of registers, and so after processing data values it can store them off into memory locations. Microcomputers possess typically several thousand memory locations, which are used for holding such data values and also the set of "program instructions" which are to be obeyed. An instruction is therefore a multi-bit bit pattern (or "word"). It is often impossible to tell by cursory examination of a microcomputer's memory whether blocks of words represent instructions, which the machine fetches and implements in turn, or data values, which it processes (e.g. using arithmetic and logic operations) in its registers.

1.4 INTEGRATED CIRCUITS

Until the 1970s gates, registers and larger functional modules within computers were constructed using discrete component transistors, resistors and other devices. Such circuits were physically large and consumed high electrical power. Large circuit functions comprising tens of thousands of transistors are now built into single electronic packages called "integrated circuits".

The standard packaging device is the DIL (dual-in-line) package, as shown in Fig. 1.5. In this device the silicon wafer, into which is built the large number of transistor circuits, is connected to the external connection pins by means of fine gold wires.

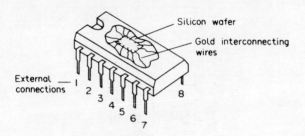

FIG. 1.5. DIL integrated circuit.

Integrated circuits, or ICs, are generally from 8 to 40 pin units, and perform a wide range of digital circuit functions. Even analogue circuits, e.g. amplifiers, are also available in ICs.

There are three common families of ICs, as follows.

(a) TTL (Transistor Transistor Logic)

Although one of the first of the circuit construction techniques for ICs, or "chips", TTL still survives as one of the most widely used. It possesses one powerful advantage over other families: speed of operation. Although TTL ICs are found in microcomputer circuits, they are not used for the high-density kernel modules of microprocessor, memory, etc. They consume too much electrical power for such functions, and their packing density is too low. They are built using only "medium scale integration" (MSI) with typically 100 components per chip. However, they are useful devices for performing simple gating functions, as shown in Fig. 1.6. The 14-pin package provides four fast-switching NAND gates. The DC supply voltage enters on pins 7 and 14. Notice the notch which is cut on one edge of the chip; this is used as an alignment marker so that pin numbers can be identified.

TTL circuits, which consist of only transistors and resistors, are created on a circular wafer of pure silicon using a process of masking and diffusion to "dope" certain areas of the crystal with impurities. These areas form the different sections of individual transistors and resistors. The entire wafer is scribed and cut into individual chips, which are then mounted in their dual-in-line packages.

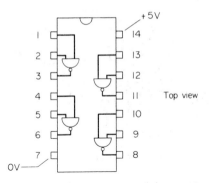

FIG. 1.6. TTL 74LS00 quad NAND gate IC.

(b) MOS (Metal Oxide Semiconductor)

The development of MOS circuits in the Santa Clara ("silicon") Valley in California in the late 1960s and 1970s has led to the introduction of microcomputers which consist of a handful of chips. MOS circuits enable up to 100,000 transistors using VLSI (Very Large Scale Integration) to be built into a single chip. Only transistors are used to construct such circuits—the elimination of resistors has led to the extremely high packing densities. A new type of transistor, the unipolar FET (Field Effect Transistor), is used in MOS circuits in place of the conventional bipolar transistor.

Most microprocessor, memory and intelligent input/output chips are manufactured using MOS technology. Two sub-divisions of MOS are applied—PMOS was used with the first microprocessors but has been superceded by NMOS, which is faster.

The advantages of MOS over TTL and discrete component circuits are packing density, cost, lower power consumption (e.g. 0.1 mW per gate for MOS c.f. 10 mW per gate for TTL) and reliability. However, they are slower in operation.

(c) CMOS (Complementary MOS)

CMOS is a variation of the generalised MOS family, but it is worthy of

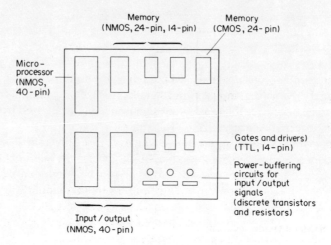

FIG. 1.7. Typical microcomputer board layout.

separate consideration. Two different types of FETs are used in its construction; hence the name complementary.

A CMOS chip offers even greater packing density than MOS, and CMOS devices are beginning to challenge the traditional MOS applications for memory devices and even microprocessors. Its extremely low power consumption (e.g. 10 nW per gate c.f. 0.1 mW per gate for MOS) and high levels of circuit integration guarantee its future role in microelectronic systems.

CMOS does present a special problem due to its susceptibility to static voltages. Chips can be damaged by discharge of static voltages which are caused by careless handling.

The advent of integrated circuits has introduced an advantage which is additional to the size reduction of electronic circuits and the resulting implementation of a complete digital computer onto a single chip or a small number of chips. This additional advantage is that the task of the system designer is much eased. A single chip performs a large modular function of the overall circuit, and the design role is reduced to one of merely arranging for the correct interconnection of a small number of high-integration chips.

Figure 1.7 shows a typical board layout for a small microcomputer. The microprocessor is normally a 40-pin IC, and could be an 8-bit or a 16-bit device. Memory is normally NMOS, and can be read-only (ROM) or read-and-write (RAM). Input/output ICs are often intelligent and flexible in operation; 40-pin packages are common for chips which provide a large number of input/output signals. TTL circuits are used for simple gating and signal driving (e.g. input/output signals) roles. Conventional transistors may be necessary if large current signals need to be carried from the board to external devices.

In some large volume applications, which require only a small amount of memory and a limited number of input/output signals, the functions of microprocessor, memory and input/output can be combined within a single chip. Examples of single-chip microcomputer applications are digital watch, pocket game, washing machine controller, etc.

This particular book emphasises input/output chips and circuits and their role in interfacing microcomputers to remote peripherals and devices. However, it would not be complete without a list of the main microprocessor types as follows:

8-bit microprocessors	16-bit microprocessors
Intel 8080 (2 chips)	Texas Instruments 9900
Intel 8085	Intel 8088
Zilog Z80	Intel 8086
MOS Technology 6502	Zilog Z8001
Motorola 6800	Motorola 68000
	National Semiconductor 16000

Arguably the most powerful devices in each category are the Z80 and the 68000.

BIBLIOGRAPHY

1. *Microelectronic Systems 1 Checkbook*. R. E. Vears, Butterworths, 1981.
2. *Microprocessor Appreciation*. Glyn Martin, Hutchinson, 1982.

CHAPTER 2

Microcomputer Construction

2.1 MICROCOMPUTER APPLICATIONS

Microcomputers are constructed using a small number of micro-electronic components. Applications of microcomputers have extended rapidly as the size and cost of these components have tumbled over the last few years. A large industrial plant logging and control microcomputer may cost £20,000, whilst a digital watch, which is controlled by a single-chip microcomputer, can be purchased for £3 (the actual chip costs far less). Figure 2.1 shows typical microcomputer systems over a wide range of applications.

Mass-produced consumer items such as digital watches, clock pens, pocket calculators and hand-held games normally consist of a single-chip circuit. A washing machine controller or a petrol pump controller contains more circuitry to enable it to interface with a wide range of electrical devices (motor, heater, solenoid valves). The largest microcomputer systems, i.e. office computer (including word processor) and plant logger, contain several circuit boards, which fit into a mother-board, and require fairly large power supplies.

In summary, the proliferation of the use of microelectronic circuits has been staggering. In the future, microcomputers will be used increasingly in the home, office and factory. Traditional electromechanical and electronic products will be replaced by microcomputer solutions, and the advantages of cost and size will enable new products to be introduced.

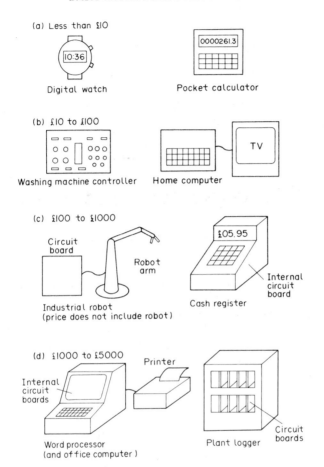

FIG. 2.1. Typical microcomputer applications.

2.2 BASIC MICROCOMPUTER CIRCUIT

Every microcomputer circuit can be reduced to the functional modules shown in Fig. 2.2. In the smallest and low-powered applications, such as

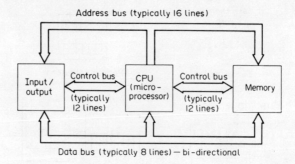

Address bus (typically 16 lines)

FIG. 2.2. Simplified diagram of microcomputer.

digital watch or clock, these three modules are combined into a single chip. Normally the microprocessor or CPU (Central Processor Unit) is a single-chip 40-pin IC, whilst there may be several ICs forming each of the memory and input/output circuits. In this latter arrangement the three "buses" perform the following functions:

(a) *Data bus*—This carries a program instruction (i.e. a specific operation which the CPU is to perform) into the CPU, or it carries a data item between the CPU and memory or input/output. In an 8-bit microprocessor this bus consists of 8 lines.

(b) *Address bus*—This carries the memory or input/output address of the data item or program instruction (from memory only) which is carried along the data bus. Commonly this bus has 16 lines to give 64K addresses (1K = 1024).

(c) *Control bus*—This is a collection of timing and control signals which supervise the above actions.

Consider the simplest arrangement of a 3-chip system consisting of a CPU (8-bit device), a single memory IC and a single input/output IC. The CPU continually transfers program instructions in 8-bit (byte) groups from memory and examines and executes these instructions within the CPU. Occasionally an input/output operation may be demanded in one of the instructions. In this case the CPU uses the three buses to transfer data

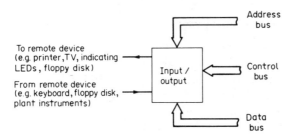

FIG. 2.3. Typical input/output connections.

to or from the input/output IC. Connection to remote devices from this IC is shown in Fig. 2.3. Most microprocessor manufacturers offer one or two standardised input/output chips which can be used to connect to several different type of devices listed in this diagram. Additionally specialised input/output ICs are available to perform sophisticated input/output duties, e.g. a single chip can be used to control a floppy disk unit. These ranges of ICs, and the circuits which connect to them, are the detailed subject of this text. Firstly, in the remaining part of this chapter, we will examine the main elements of the CPU and memory components within the basic microcomputer.

2.3 CPU (CENTRAL PROCESSOR UNIT)

Detailed diagrams of a typical CPU or microprocessor are shown in Fig. 2.4.

The great majority of microprocessors are 40-pin ICs, as shown in Fig. 2.4(a). Whilst the actual pin numbers, which are assigned to the various signals, vary from one CPU to another, the same groups of signals are apparent. Apart from the three buses (data, address and control), additional connections are required for DC power (+5 V and 0 V—occasionally an additional +12 V or −12 V is required) and a crystal clock. This clock initiates and times all of the CPU's activities.

The internal operation of the CPU is demonstrated in Fig. 2.4(b). The modules which are shown perform the following functions.

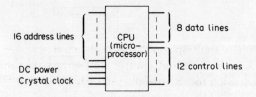

(a) Physical construction (40-pin IC)

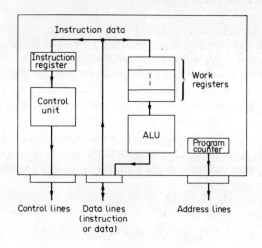

(b) Internal organisation

Fig. 2.4. CPU (microprocessor).

(a) Program Counter

This holds the address of the next program instruction which is to be fetched from memory.

(b) Instruction Register

This holds the instruction which the CPU is obeying currently.

(c) Control Unit

This unit examines and implements the instruction which is held in the instruction register. It sends out control signals around the CPU (and beyond the CPU, using the control bus) in order to execute the instruction.

(d) ALU (Arithmetic and Logic Unit)

The ALU performs any arithmetic (e.g. add, subtract) or data manipulation (e.g. invert all bits, rotate or shift a data item one place to the left, etc.) which may be required by an instruction.

(e) Work Registers

These provide temporary storage of data items which are being processed in a program of instructions. Different microprocessors describe them commonly by:

(1) letter, e.g. A, B, C, D, E, H and L;

(2) number, e.g. R0, R1, R2, etc.

The former method is more common. Normally one particular register, which is generally known as the accumulator (or A register), is the only one which receives the result of ALU operations. Thus the CPU can only add into the accumulator (register A) and not register B, or any other.

The basic operation of the CPU can be summarised in the following few sentences. The CPU extracts one program instruction at a time from memory, places that instruction in its instruction register and then implements it. After each instruction the program counter is incremented automatically to point to the address of the next instruction in memory. The control unit, which is triggered and timed by the CPU crystal clock (typically 2 MHz), initiates each action in the implementation of each instruction. If an instruction requires some activity from the ALU, the control unit selects that function and gates data items through the ALU at the correct time. Therefore, the control unit examines the instruction in the instruction register and sends out control signals to implement it.

A description of the detailed operation of a sample instruction may help the reader to appreciate the functions of these various modules. Consider the following instruction:

ADI 5   Add (immediate) 5 to the accumulator

This is a two-byte instruction, i.e. it is stored in two consecutive bytes of memory—some instructions are one-byte and others are three-byte.

The procedure for the implementation of each instruction follows the "fetch-execute" cycle, i.e. firstly the instruction is fetched from memory, and then it is executed. Figure 2.5 shows these two stages for the case of our sample instruction. Assume that initially (as a result of previous program actions) the accumulator holds 03, and that the instruction is held in memory locations hex. 20A3 and 20A4.

The fetch part of the sequence is the same for every instruction. The control unit gates out the contents of the program counter (hex. 20A3) onto the address bus. The first byte (the "opcode"—C6 in this case) is passed into the CPU and placed in the instruction register. In the execute part of the instruction the control unit examines the opcode, and in this case gates in the contents of the next byte in memory (05). Simultaneously the control unit gates this value and the contents of the accumulator through the ALU, which it sets to perform an add operation. The answer (08) is passed back into the accumulator and overwrites the previous contents (03).

At the end of the instruction the program counter is incremented to 20A5 to point to the memory address of the next instruction.

The reader may like to test his understanding of the fetch-execute cycle by analysing the following examples, possibly by sketching the contents of the CPU modules at various stages (as in Fig. 2.5).

EXAMPLE 1

MVI B,23H   Move (immediate) hex. 23 into B register

This two-byte instruction is 06 and 23, and it resides in memory locations 10C3 and 10C4.

The stages are:

(a) Fetch.

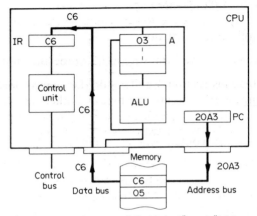

(a) Instruction fetch – read first byte ("opcode") into instruction register

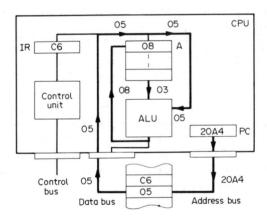

(b) Instruction execute – read second byte from memory and add to accumulator

FIG. 2.5. Fetch-execute cycle for ADI 5 (add 5 to accumulator).

(b) Execute—transfer hex. 23 from second byte of instruction in memory to the B register.

EXAMPLE 2

RLC   Rotate contents of A register (accumulator) left 1 place

This single-byte instruction is 07, and it resides at memory location 00E9. The stages are:

(a) Fetch.
(b) Execute—pass contents of accumulator (04 initially) through ALU, shift left 1 place and return number to accumulator.

What does the accumulator hold finally? What is the relationship between the initial and final numbers? (Answers at end of chapter.)

EXAMPLE 3

JMP 4C00H   Jump to instruction at memory location hex. 4C00

This triple-byte instruction is C3, 00 and 4C, and it resides at memory locations 384E, 384F and 3850. The stages are:

(a) Fetch.
(b) Execute 1—read in next byte of instruction (lower-order half of address 4C00) into half of temporary register (one of work registers).
(c) Execute 2—read in last byte of instruction (higher-order half of address 4C00) into the other half of temporary register, and transfer contents of this temporary register to program counter.

2.4 MEMORY

There are two types of semiconductor memory:

(a) ROM—"read only memory", i.e. once program instructions and data items are initially written into the device, they can only be read.

(b) RAM—literally this is "random access memory", but a better description is "read and write memory", i.e. instructions and data items can be read from and written back into RAM.

Most microcomputers possess some ROM and some RAM. A drawback with RAM is that whenever DC is removed, e.g. the microcomputer is switched off, all contents are lost. Therefore ROM is normally used to hold programs which are required at switch-on and which will never need to be altered.

There are three types of ROM:

(a) ROM—read only memory (programmed by chip manufacturer).
(b) PROM—programmable ROM (i.e. the user can program the device).
(c) EPROM—erasable PROM (i.e. the user can program the device, erase it using a UV, i.e. ultra-violet, light source, and re-program it repeatedly).

Figure 2.6 shows a typical ROM device. DC supply connections are not shown—this is normal in circuit diagrams. Notice the following features:

(1) 12 address lines—12 lines give 2^{12} ($=2048$) locations.
(2) 8 data lines—8 lines give 8 bits (1 byte) storage in each location.
(3) 1 chip select—this signal activates the device, i.e. data is only presented on the data lines (from the address which enters on the address lines) when the chip select is set.

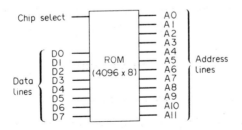

FIG. 2.6. ROM chip (4K bytes). 1K = 1024.

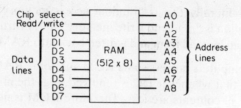

FIG. 2.7. RAM chip (512 bytes).

Figure 2.7 shows a typical RAM chip. Notice the following features:

(1) 9 address lines—9 lines give 2^9 ($=512$) locations.
(2) 8 data lines—as for ROM.
(3) 1 chip select—as for ROM.
(4) 1 read/write—this control bus signal determines whether the selected storage byte (determined by address lines) is to be read from or written to.

There is one complication with the construction of most RAM ICs. They do not normally possess 8 data pins, i.e. they do not provide byte storage. "Static" RAM ICs are commonly 4-bit devices, and "dynamic" RAM ICs are often 1-bit devices (the reader is referred to most standard textbooks on microcomputer technology for a detailed description of these two types of RAM, if required). Figure 2.8 shows how two 4-bit RAMs are

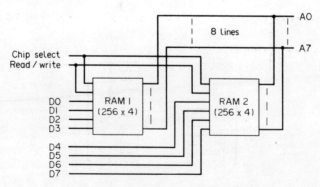

FIG. 2.8. RAM pair (to provide byte storage).

combined to give byte storage, i.e. one-half of the data bus is connected to each chip. The chip select signal activates both chips simultaneously and the read/write signal sets both chips to the read or write state.

It is not difficult to visualise the circuit arrangement for 1-bit RAM ICs, i.e. 8 off 1-bit ICs are connected to the data bus in order to provide the standard byte storage, and they all share the same chip select and read/write signals.

2.5 ADDRESS DECODING

Before we can analyse input/output circuit arrangements in more detail, it is necessary to examine the technique which is applied to both memory and input/output circuits in microcomputers in order to ensure that only one memory or input/output IC is selected at a time. This is necessary so that the microprocessor does not attempt to transfer data to or from more than a single IC.

The technique which is applied is demonstrated in Fig. 2.9. A 2 to 4 decoder IC possesses the characteristic of setting only one of its outputs at any time. The particular output which is set is determined by the setting of the two inputs. The truth table details these combinations. If the two

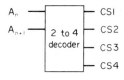

(a) Circuit symbol

A_{n+1}	A_n	CS4	CS3	CS2	CS1
0	0	0	0	0	1
0	1	0	0	1	0
1	0	0	1	0	0
1	1	1	0	0	0

(b) Truth table

FIG. 2.9. 2 to 4 decoder.

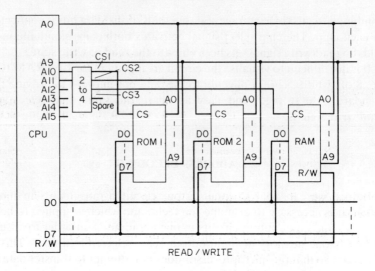

Fig. 2.10. Microcomputer circuit diagram (CPU and memory).

inputs are connected to two unused high-order address lines, then the outputs can be used to connect to the chip select pins on individual memory or input/output ICs. Thus only one IC is active at any time. Each memory and input/output chip is "tri-state", i.e. its data pins, which connect to the data bus, can be set to three states—1, 0 and "floating". When the chip select signal is not set for the device, its data connections are in the floating state. The address decoding circuit within a micro-computer ensures that only one device takes the data bus out of the floating state therefore.

Figure 2.10 shows the full circuit arrangement which can be used to connect a microprocessor to a memory circuit which includes some ROM and RAM chips, and also demonstrates the application of a 2 to 4 decoder. For simplicity ROM1, ROM2 and the RAM chip are all 1024×8 devices (the reader may like to check that the correct number of address lines are connected). The 2 to 4 decoder generates the chip select signals for each of the ICs. The address of the first location in each of these devices is computed from Table 2.1.

TABLE 2.1. START ADDRESSES FOR THE
MEMORY ICs IN FIG. 2.10

	A15 A14 A13 A12	A11 A10	A9 A8 A7 A6 A5 A4 A3 A2 A1 A0	Hex.
ROM1	— — — —	0 0	0 0 0 0 0 0 0 0 0 0	0000
ROM2	— — — —	0 1	0 0 0 0 0 0 0 0 0 0	0400
RAM	— — — —	1 0	0 0 0 0 0 0 0 0 0 0	0800
Spare	— — — —	1 1	0 0 0 0 0 0 0 0 0 0	0C00

Not connected   2 to 4   ↑
(say all 0s)   decoder   Start
address

For example, if the following instruction is executed by the micro-processor:

LDA 0403H   Load accumulator with the contents of memory location hex. 0403

then the fourth byte in ROM2 is selected.

Notice that in this circuit only one control bus signal (Read/Write) is connected to the memory circuit. Also observe that only 9 address lines (A0 to A8) would need to be connected to the RAM IC if it is a 512-byte device.

If more than four memory ICs are used in a circuit, then two 2 to 4 decoders, or a 3 to 8 decoder, are necessary. The reader may like to draw out the circuit symbol and truth table for the latter device.

The same address decoding technique is used for input/output circuits. Figure 2.11 shows a circuit in which three simple input/output chips are used. Notice that there are no address lines taken to each of these input/output ICs. Thus each chip possesses a single address (00, 01 or 02—as determined by the 2 to 4 decoder circuit). Therefore, the following instruction:

OUT 01H   Output contents of accumulator to input/output address 01

outputs 8 bits through input/output 2 chip, which may be connected to a printer, a group of 8 indicating lamps, etc.

A method of ensuring that only one of a group of memory ICs *or* one of

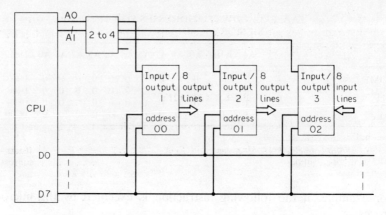

Fig. 2.11. Microcomputer circuit diagram (CPU and input/output).

a group of input/output ICs is selected is shown in Fig. 2.12. Whenever an input or an output instruction (rather than a memory transfer instruction) is executed, the control bus signal input/output selected is set. This is used to perform a chip select function on the 2 to 4 decoder ICs. For example, if an input instruction is executed the top 2 to 4 decoder is selected; the bottom 2 to 4 decoder is not selected, and this means that none of its four outputs (CS5 to CS8) can be set.

The reader may like to exercise his understanding of these techniques by sketching out the full circuit diagram for a simple microcomputer which comprises several memory and several input/output ICs.

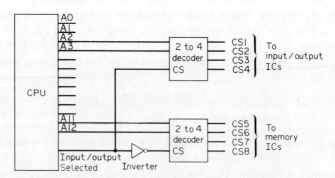

Fig. 2.12. Circuit technique to select only memory or input/output.

(*Answer*: 08. This is double the original number. Therefore the shift or rotate instruction has multiplied the original number by 2; shifting left by 2 places multiplies the number by 4, and so on.)

BIBLIOGRAPHY

1. *Basic Principles and Practice of Microprocessors*. D. E. Heffer, G. A. King and D. Keith, Edward Arnold, 1980.
2. *Study Notes for Technicians. Microelectronic Systems Levels 1 and 2*. R. C. Holland, McGraw-Hill, 1983.
3. *Microcomputer Primer*. Mitchell Waite and Michael Pardee, Sams, 1980.

CHAPTER 3

Principal Input/Output ICs

3.1 PARALLEL INPUT/OUTPUT (THE PIO)

Invariably microprocessor manufacturers support their CPU chips with a parallel input/output (PIO) IC. Usually this device is also 40-pin and can cost as much as the microprocessor itself. However, it is a powerful and flexible component, which can enable connection to be made to a wide range of remote devices. The device can be programmed to perform input *or* output functions, or some combination of both.

Figure 3.1 shows the typical circuit arrangement with a PIO. The connections are as follows:

(a) Chip select (generated by a 2 to 4 or a 3 to 8 decoder).
(b) Read/write (this is a control bus line which is used to distinguish between input and output instructions).
(c) Address lines (3 address lines give a possible 8 individual addresses on the IC—Port A, Port B, Port C, two others to be explained later, and three unused).
(d) Data lines (normal 8 bits from data bus).
(e) Two or three ports (a port is an 8-bit input/output channel; notice that if a third port is available it is often reduced to a 6-bit channel).

Each port can be used to connect to remote peripherals, e.g. printer, keyboard, or to groups of discrete signals, e.g. indicating LEDs (light emitting diodes), lamps, switches, etc. Any additional circuitry which is required for these applications is described later.

Each port possesses a different address, e.g. 01, 02 and 03. An

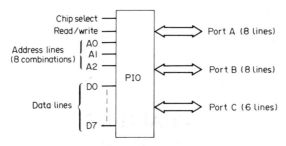

FIG. 3.1. Typical PIO (Programmable Input/Output).

additional address is used for a "control register", which is the mechanism by which the programmable feature of the device is obtained. The device can be "programmed" to set its ports as either input or output by sending special control bytes to the control register. This is performed by software before the main input/output program in the microcomputer attempts to use the ports. Once the control register has been used to identify the "directions" of the ports, they are fixed as input or output ports until reprogrammed or until the machine is switched off. Frequently ports default to become output ports after DC is first applied at machine switch-on.

An example of this "initialising" procedure, i.e. select direction of ports, is as follows:

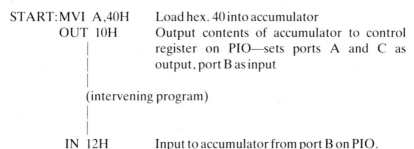

```
START: MVI  A,40H      Load hex. 40 into accumulator
       OUT  10H        Output contents of accumulator to control
        |              register on PIO—sets ports A and C as
        |              output, port B as input
        |
       (intervening program)
        |
        |
       IN   12H        Input to accumulator from port B on PIO.
```

The output (OUT) instruction sends a control byte of hex. 40 to the control register, which has an address of hex. 10. This control byte initialises the PIO such that port B (address hex. 12) is the only input port.

The addresses on the device are therefore:

    10 = control register
    11 = port A (output)
    12 = port B (input)
    13 = port C (output)

It is necessary to examine the manufacturer's data sheets for a PIO to determine the precise control bit pattern which must be sent to the device to set the ports to the required configuration. Sections 8.2, 9.2 and 10.2 describe the initialising procedure for the PIOs manufactured by Intel, Zilog and Texas Instruments.

Most PIOs offer a facility which is additional to the primary function of providing input/output ports. A counter/timer circuit is included within the IC, and this can be used by the microprocessor, and the program which is obeyed, for a variety of applications.

Figure 3.2 shows the additional signals which are associated with this counter/timer circuit. Clock pulses, which are normally generated by the CPU (divided down from its high frequency crystal-controlled input clock, e.g. 2 Mhz), are used to decrement the counter. Additionally a count complete signal is generated when the counter reaches zero. The ways in which a counter/timer circuit is used are as follows:

(a) Interval Timer

Consider the arrangement shown in Fig. 3.2. If a count is output from the CPU and placed in the counter, then a fixed period elapses before the clock pulses decrement the counter setting to zero. The count complete signal can be "polled", or continuously checked, within the program until it is set when the counter reaches zero. At this point the program scan can cease and a *precise* program delay has been achieved.

If the addresses on the PIO are:

    10 = control register
    11 = port A
    12 = port B
    13 = port C
    14 = counter/timer

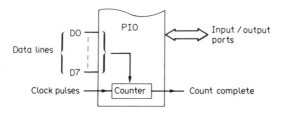

FIG. 3.2. Counter/timer section of PIO.

and the clock pulses are set at 0.5 μsec (1 μsec $= 10^{-6}$ sec), then the following program generates a delay of 200 $\times$ 0.5 μsec $= 0.1$ msec (10^{-4} sec)

MVI	A,200	Load decimal 200 into accumulator
OUT	14H	Output contents of accumulator to counter
POLL:IN	10H	Input control register setting to accumulator
ANI	20H	Exclude all bits except count complete
JZ	POLL	Jump back if count complete is not set

The count complete is set as one bit in the control register. The ANI (AND immediate) instruction is a "masking" instruction, i.e. it sets all bits to zero except for the single bit which is in the position of the 1 in 0010 0000 (hex. 20). The final instruction means "jump if zero", and it causes a program loop to cycle continuously until the count is complete, i.e. when 0.1 msec has elapsed.

(b) Regular Interrupt Pulses

The same arrangement is used in this case, except that the count complete signal is not polled. Instead the program continues and obeys some alternative function until the count complete signal is set. The signal is connected to an "interrupt" line, which forms part of the control bus. When the signal is set the main program stops and a special interrupt service program is entered. Typically this program increments a count in memory, and when the interrupt program is completed the main program is re-entered. Additionally the counter resets itself and commences to count down once more. In this way a continuous stream of pulses is generated on the count complete signal line, and therefore the interrupt program is called on a regular basis.

The advantage of this arrangement is that the count which is incremented in memory by the interrupt service program can represent the time-of-day, as follows:

(1) tenths of seconds
(2) seconds
(3) tens of seconds
(4) minutes   } each count is held in a separate
(5) tens of minutes   memory location
(6) hours
(7) tens of hours

For example, Fig. 3.3 shows how a counter/timer count complete signal initiates an interrupt program which increments a series of counts (in memory) which represent the time-of-day. A main program also accesses these counts, and it sends them through input/output ports (perhaps on the same PIO) to drive a numerical display. Thus we have the design for a microcomputer-based digital clock.

The microcomputer's knowledge of the time-of-day need not be limited

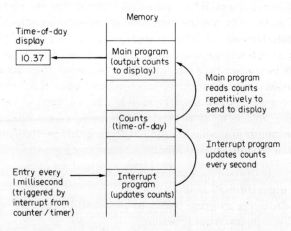

FIG. 3.3. Memory map of interrupt-driven real-time-clock.

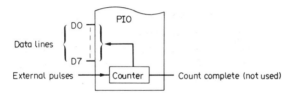

FIG. 3.4. Use of counter/timer to count external pulses.

to a display function. Additionally the interrupt program could call other programs at specific times, e.g. a print program could be called every hour to present a data summary on a printer. Alternatively, a program could be called at regular intervals, e.g. a plant instrumentation scanning program could be called every 10 sec.

The reader is referred to section 7.4 if difficulty is experienced in understanding the microprocessor's response on receiving an interrupt signal.

(c) Event Counter

Sometimes a microcomputer is required to count external events, and each event is represented by a voltage pulse, e.g. an object intercepting a beam of light. The easiest method of performing this function is demonstrated in Fig. 3.4. The external pulses replace the CPU clock and the count complete is not used in this arrangement. Also the counter is set to increment (rather than decrement) by software "initialisation". The external pulses increment the counter, which can be read into the CPU. Also the counter can be reset to zero by the software to initiate a new count.

This technique is easier to apply and presents fewer software "overheads" than the following alternatives:

(1) Repeatedly poll the external pulses which are connected as a single bit input through an input port.
(2) Connect the external pulses to an interrupt line and service each pulse in an interrupt program.

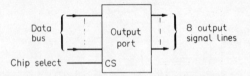

FIG. 3.5. Single port output (non-programmable).

3.2 NON-PROGRAMMABLE INPUT/OUTPUT PORTS

Following that detailed analysis of PIOs and their powerful range of facilities, a simpler but less-flexible device is worthy of examination. If a port is to be fixed as an input or an output port, i.e. the programmable feature is not required, then the device shown in Fig. 3.5 represents a simpler and cheaper alternative. In this straightforward circuit no address lines are connected since there are no addresses on the chip—when the chip select is set by an address decoder, the data bus is passed through to the 8 ouput lines which feed to a remote device. Notice that in this case, as for ports from a PIO, the settings of the 8 output pins are "latched", i.e. once set to 1s and 0s they are held at these levels permanently until changed by a later output instruction.

Clearly the diagram for a single input port IC is the same except that the directions are reversed.

A typical IC of this type is the 74373, which can be used as either an input or an output port, and is often described as an "octal (8-bit) latch". Its circuit connections as both port types are shown in Fig. 3.6. Data passes through the device only when CS (chip select) is set to 1 and $\overline{O\,E}$ (output enable—inverse logic) is set to 0. Thus in circuit (a) $\overline{O\,E}$ is set permanently, and the address decoder signal activates the device through CS. In circuit (b) CS is set permanently, and the address decoder signal (which must go to 0) activates the device through $\overline{O\,E}$.

An alternative device is the Intel 8212.

3.3 SERIAL INPUT/OUTPUT (THE UART)

In the devices described in sections 3.1 and 3.2 data is transferred in

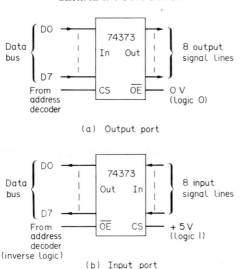

(a) Output port

(b) Input port

Fig. 3.6. Use of 8-bit latch IC as output and input port.

parallel form, i.e. each bit is set on a discrete signal line and all bits are set simultaneously. This is the normal method of data connection between microcomputers and remote devices and peripherals. However, an alternative form of data transfer is often used, and this is termed serial transmission. In this system data bits are transferred one after the other along a single signal connection. The advantage which serial transmission gives is that only two wires (one for signal, one for a reference 0 V) are required to connect a microcomputer to a remote peripheral, e.g. a printer, VDU or another computer. Parallel communication requires 9 wires (8 for data bits, 1 for reference 0 V) since data is normally transferred in 8-bit (byte) groups. However data transfer is slower with serial communication.

The IC which is used to provide serial data transfer is the UART (Universal Asynchronous Receiver/Transmitter), as shown in Fig. 3.7. The device is connected to both the data bus (D0–D7) and to the output of an address decoder circuit (chip select) in the same manner as for a PIO. Additionally the read/write control bus signal is connected to select input or output. A clock pulse, which is often a derivation of the CPU

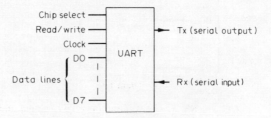

FIG. 3.7. Typical UART.

clock, is required to pulse data in and out. A UART is always bidirectional, i.e. a Tx (transmit) and Rx (receive) channel are provided.

The word "asynchronous" means that no synchronising clock is required between a UART at each end of the data link. Synchronous links are rarely used, however a USART (Universal Synchronous *and* Asynchronous Receiver/Transmiter) device is fairly common, but it is invariably used only in the asynchronous mode.

Figure 3.8 shows the method of connection from a microcomputer to a VDU (Visual Display Unit), which is the standard operator interface peripheral device. The UART in each device performs serial-to-parallel and parallel-to-serial conversion.

The reader can readily identify the method of connection from one microcomputer to another. The Tx from one UART is connected to the

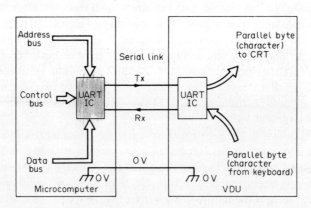

FIG. 3.8. Microcomputer to VDU serial link.

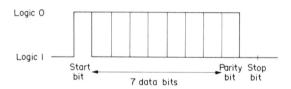

FIG. 3.9. RS 232-C waveform for serial communication.

Rx on the other UART, and vice versa. Similarly the serial connection to a printer involves only the Tx connection (plus 0 V reference).

Data transfer for serial communication conforms to the RS 232-C standard (or its updated equivalent the RS 422). This is a world-standard specification for signal requirements for serial links, and the signal waveform for the transfer of one byte, or character, is shown in Fig. 3.9. The seven data bits plus parity bit comprise an alphabet character which can be a letter, number or a special control character. The bit pattern for each character is invariably specified by the ASCII (American Standard Code for Information Interchange) code. This code is listed in the Appendix. The 8-bit character is framed by a start bit (logic 0) and a stop bit (logic 1).

Between characters the signal line is held at logic 1.

The most important features of the RS 232-C standard are as follow.

(a) Speed

The signal transmission speed is defined as "baud rate" (bits per second). Standard speeds are 110, 300, 1200, 2400, 4800 and 9600 baud. However, some recent UARTs will transfer at even higher rates (multiples of the above speeds). For example, a drive to a printer at 600 baud enables 60 characters/second to be printed—each character requires 10 bits (including start and stop bits).

(b) Signal Levels

Logic 1 = approximately −9 V (−3 V to −15 V)
Logic 0 = approximately +9 V (+3 V to +15 V)

(c) Pin Connections

The signal connections are brought to an interconnection plug, which is normally of the 25-pin "D"-type, or Cannon-type. The following pin connections are used:

$$Tx = \text{pin } 2$$
$$Rx = \text{pin } 3 \Big\} \text{ data connections}$$
$$0\,V = \text{pin } 7$$

$$RTS\,(\text{request to send}) = \text{pin } 4$$
$$CTS\,(\text{clear to send}) = \text{pin } 5$$

control signals to perform "hand-shaking" between two UARTs—often connect together ("back-to-back") on same UART

(d) Parity Checking

If even parity is selected for the link, then the transmitting UART must count the number of 1s in the 7 data bits and set a 1 in the parity bit if that number is odd (e.g. 1, 3, 5 or 7) in order to achieve an overall even parity. The reverse applies for odd parity.

Therefore, a UART is set to operate in one of the several optional modes, as follows:

(1) baud rate—for both Tx and Rx (they can be different)
(2) number of data bits—normally 7 (but could be different)
(3) number of stop bits—normally 1 (but could be 2 or even $1\frac{1}{2}$)
(4) parity—even or odd.

Sometimes these options can be selected by setting switches which connect signal levels to the UART to specify the required modes. However it is more common, and certainly more flexible, to find that a UART is "programmable" in much the same way as for a PIO. Software can send control bytes to such a UART to "initialise" the device to set its baud rate, parity, etc.

Two variations of the three-wire interconnection system can occur. Firstly if a VDU, or "terminal", is sited several kilometres from its driving computer, the interconnections which are used are generally spare conductors in a telephone cable. However, long distance transmission causes the transmitted pulses to become distorted due to cable capacitance. Additionally the telephone network, particularly if repeaters or amplifiers are encountered, is designed to handle sinewaves for speech signals. Therefore a modem is required at each end of the link to handle the conversion between pulses and sinewaves of different frequencies (e.g. 1 = 1270 Hz, 0 = 1070 Hz).

Secondly "current loop" signals are sometimes used in place of the voltage signal levels (+9 V and −9 V). In this arrangement logic 1 is represented by 20 mA (milliamps) and logic 0 by 0 mA. Although additional circuitry is required beyond the UART to generate these signals, longer distance transmission can be achieved. Often baud rates have to be reduced to achieve successful data transfer over long links. The complete update of a VDU screen (e.g. 2000 characters) at 4800 baud (480 characters/second) takes approximately 4 seconds. Halving the baud rate doubles this time to 8 seconds, which can prove annoying to an operator. Therefore speed optimisation can be important.

At the start of this section it was stated that serial communication is used between microcomputers and printers, VDUs and other computers. However, many printers offer both a serial and parallel interface. The principal advantage (reduced number of interconnecting cable cores) which serial links offer was exploited traditionally by mainframe and minicomputers. These machines often drive large numbers of printers which can be distributed widely throughout a building and beyond. However, a microcomputer normally drives a single printer, which is located adjacent to the machine, and so the saving in cable cores is of little significance. Hence parallel drive to a printer is extremely common with microcomputers, and a single 8-bit port is used. This is often described as a "Centronics" interface, because the most popular printer which was connected initially by parallel link to a microcomputer was manufactured by Centronics. In addition to the simple 8-bit output port, two additional handshaking signals are applied with the Centronics interface—Strobe (output signal from microcomputer) and Acknowledge (reply from printer).

BIBLIOGRAPHY

1. *From Chips to Systems: An Introduction to Microprocessors*. Rodnay Zaks. Sybex, 1981.
2. *Microprocessors and Microcomputers*. B. G. Woollard. McGraw-Hill, 1981.

CHAPTER 4

Digital Interfacing Techniques

4.1 DIGITAL OUTPUTS

In the previous chapter we examined the role of parallel and serial ICs in transferring data into and out from a microcomputer. In a future chapter we will investigate specialised input/output ICs which communicate with specific peripherals, e.g. floppy disks. However, we now need to examine the circuits and devices which utilise the parallel ports for data transfer. It is this area which is the most diverse, and perhaps the most interesting, in the interfacing field. Serial communication using UARTs, which has already been described, is stereotyped and is the common technique for interfacing VDUs, printers (although sometimes parallel connection is used) and other computers.

In this chapter we will explore applications for "digital inputs and outputs", i.e. signals which are set discretely to 1s and 0s, as distinct from "analogue signals", e.g. instrumentation readings.

Figure 4.1 shows how simple single-bit output signals are connected to an output port. The output port could be a single chip (see 3.2) or one of the two or three ports on a PIO (see 3.1). Seven typical examples of digital output applications are shown as follows.

(a) LED (Method 1)

A LED (light emitting diode) is an extremely popular device for giving visual indication to an operator that a certain event has occurred or that a

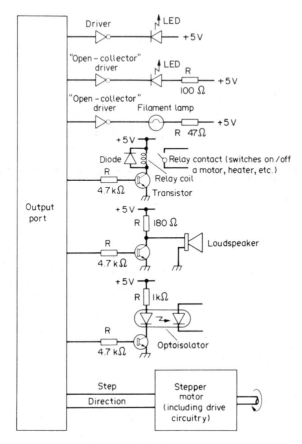

FIG. 4.1. Typical single-bit output devices.

particular device is switched on, etc. LEDs are frequently used in plant alarm/indicator panels or in consumer products. LEDs can be purchased in a variety of colours so that indication becomes more meaningful.

A LED cannot be connected directly to a port chip because insufficient current can be generated by the device, which is normally a MOS or CMOS device. A LED requires typically 20 mA (milliamps) to 80 mA, and therefore a current driver circuit must interpose the port and the

LED. Traditionally a transistor circuit would perform this role, but now one channel of a multi-bit driver IC can be used; typically six drivers are mounted on a single IC (e.g. the 7404). The circuit symbol for a driver normally includes a circle at the output (see Fig. 4.1), and this denotes bit inversion. Thus the port output signal must be set to a 1 to cause the LED to conduct and illuminate.

(b) LED (Method 2)

In this method the driver does not form a complete circuit, and is termed an "open collector" driver (e.g. the 7405—six drivers on one IC). An external resistor must be supplied, and this should feed to the +5 V rail voltage.

(c) Filament Lamp

This device is driven in the same manner as for a LED, but it normally consumes more current.

(d) Relay

If a large current must be switched by a microcomputer, e.g. a mains driven motor or heater is to be switched on/off, then an even higher drive current is required. Electrical relays can switch large currents and voltages through their contacts, which can be selected to be "normally-open" or "normally-closed". The relay coil is energised by a transistor being switched on when the port output signal is set to 1. The relay coil forms the load for the transistor; normally the coil is bridged by a reverse-biased diode which serves to eliminate the large back-emf which can be generated in the coil when it is de-energised and which could damage the transistor. Typically the relay contact switches the main voltage through to the motor/heater/fan/valve, etc., to activate the device. If an extremely large electrical load is to be switched, e.g. a hoist motor, then a second relay may be required, as shown in Fig. 4.2.

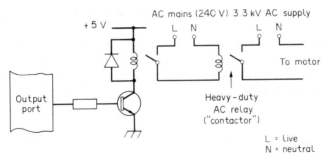

FIG. 4.2. Drive to large electrical load.

(e) Loudspeaker

The circuit connection to a louspeaker is also shown in Fig. 4.1. Once again a transistor driver is required. If a note is to be generated on the loudspeaker, clearly the software within the microcomputer must generate a signal that is closest to a sinewave, i.e. a squarewave. A squarewave is created on the output port signal line by setting it to 1, delay, setting it to 0, delay, and then repeating the sequence. The length of the software delay governs the frequency of the note.

(f) Optoisolator

A new electronic device has arrived to challenge the electrical relay in its output switching role. The optoisolator is a sealed unit which possesses two input and two output connections. Current flows between the two output connections, in one direction only, when current flows through the input connections. Although output current levels cannot be as high as through a relay contact, the device offers the same advantage of providing electrical isolation between the microcomputer circuitry and the remote device. This electrical isolation can be a useful feature if it is felt advisable for reliability and security reasons to isolate operating voltages between two circuits, e.g. a microcomputer and a remote plant control system.

(g) Stepper Motor (2 bits required)

The stepper motor has assumed a greater significance as a mechanical drive device in recent years when compared with a conventional DC motor. This is because of its signal compatibility with computers in general and microcomputers in particular. A single pulse signal is all that is required to drive the device. A second signal can be applied to select direction of rotation, if required. One pulse moves the motor by typically a few degrees of rotary motion. Therefore a specific number of pulses drives the motor shaft to a fixed position. Alternatively continuous pulses cause the motor to rotate at a speed which is determined by the pulse rate. Figure 4.1. shows the simple connection arrangement which is required to drive a stepper motor. The motor's drive circuitry is "TTL compatible", i.e. it requires the same signal characteristics that are generated by the output port. Stepper motors are used in a wide range of computer-driven applications, e.g. process control valve, robot, numerically controlled machine tool, "fruit machine" drive drum, floppy disk head drive, graph plotter, etc. For example, the connection to a stepper motor robot, which possesses six degrees of freedom (i.e. possesses six stepper motors), is shown in Fig. 4.3.

A common application of output ports is to drive numerical displays. In this case we move from a single (double for a stepper motor) signal device to one in which eight bits are normally required, since most displays are "segment" displays. The arrangement is shown in Fig. 4.4. Seven segments, plus one for decimal point, are the most common, and are adequate for displaying numbers, e.g. digital watch, pocket calculator, cash register, petrol pump display, etc. For example, the number 5 is displayed when segments a, f, g, c and d are illuminated. However, larger segment arrays are available to enable good quality letter characters to be constructed. The segments can be LCD (liquid crystal display), as shown in Fig. 4.4, which possess extremely low power consumption, or even the modern plasma display type. A popular alternative is the LED segment display, which is much brighter and more suitable for public display applications. Clearly interposing drivers are necessary for a LED segment display.

Figure 4.5 shows a multi-digit LED segment display. The four-digit display module is designed so that it does not require four separate eight-segment signals for each number, thus requiring a total of four ports (32 signals). Instead one of four "digit" lines selects a display unit which receives the segment pattern. Effectively the segment signals feed a bus

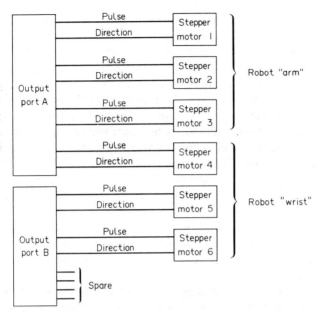

FIG. 4.3. Drive to a stepper motor robot.

within the display module and the digit 1 to digit 4 lines act as unit selection signals. Thus 1½ ports only are required to drive the complete display unit. The software which drives this arrangement must output the required segment pattern with the appropriate digit line to each of the four display units in turn.

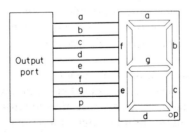

FIG. 4.4. 7-segment display (8-segment with decimal point p).

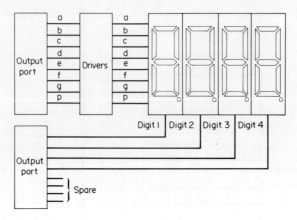

FIG. 4.5. Multi-digit LED segment display unit.

The same basic circuit can be used to drive an even larger display assembly, if an additional IC is included, as shown in Fig. 4.6. Ten display units can be selected by using only four output signals if a 4 to 10 decoder IC is used to expand the code on the four signal lines to the ten digit lines. The reader should be able to generate the truth table for a 4 to 16 decoder (see 2.5). In a 4 to 10 decoder the last six outputs are not used. The programmer must set the appropriate binary code on the output signals A, B, C and D therefore (together with the required segment pattern) when he wishes to update each of the display units.

4.2. DIGITAL INPUTS

Single-bit input signals offer less variety in terms of interfacing circuitry than digital outputs. They tend to be classified by one of the two types which are shown in Fig. 4.7. These types are "contact closure", which is more common, and voltage level. An example of the latter is a gate circuit that is switched when a light beam is detected through the transparent segments of a shaft encoder disc, which is used to indicate motor shaft position.

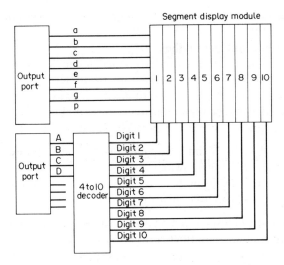

FIG. 4.6. Ten-digit segment display unit with decoder.

A remote contact closure has to be converted at the input port into a voltage level to represent a 1 or a 0 on the input signal line. This is best achieved using the resistor circuit shown. When the contact is open, the resistor clamps the input to logic 0 (0 V). When the contact closes the connection from the +5 V rail presents a logic 1, which over-rides the 0 V. The arrangement often works correctly if the resistor connection to 0 V is removed, but this is not a recommended system because when the contact is open the signal input is "floating". External electrical noise can

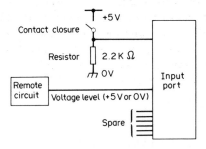

FIG. 4.7. Categories of single-bit inputs.

cause spurious 1s to be read on this signal line when it is in this state. Additionally if the input port is a CMOS device, the IC can be damaged by induced static voltages on the pin.

Contact closure signals are used to connect manually triggered signals, e.g. pushbuttons and switches, and automatically set signals, e.g. electrical relay contact and trip switches, to input ports. Manual inputs are all best connected using the top input circuit shown in Fig. 4.7, and can be of the following types:

(a) On/off switch, or similar—contact is "latched" in one position or the other, e.g. toggle switch.
(b) Pushbutton, or spring-loaded switch—contact operation is fleeting (a manual keyboard is an array of such signals).

Automatic contact closures can be from a variety of on/off transducers as shown in Fig. 4.8, and described as follows.

(a) Relay Contact

The electrical relay is an ideal interfacing device between an electrical control circuit and a microcomputer. Its contact can be used to indicate the state of conveyors, hoists, fans, pumps, motors, etc., in terms of on/off operation and position. Often spare contacts on multi-contact relays, which are used in an existing electrical system, can be utilised if a computer interface is added. Electrical isolation is maintained of course.

(b) Limit Switch

Mechanical movement can operate a range of limit or trip switches. A familiar example of this switch type is the domestic refrigerator door switch which extinguishes the internal light. Such switches can be used to indicate the position of moving vehicles, hoists, solenoids, etc.

(c) Cam Switch

Eccentric cams can be added to shafts in order to indicate rotational position by means of cam-operated switches.

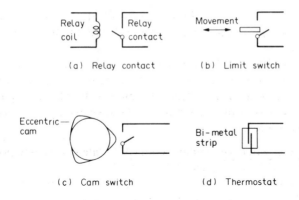

(a) Relay contact   (b) Limit switch

(c) Cam switch   (d) Thermostat

FIG. 4.8. Examples of automatic contact closure inputs.

(d) Thermostat

The widely used bi-metal strip, or thermostat, is a device which provides contact closure when the operating temperature passes a predetermined value.

These are examples of contact closures which are triggered by mechanical movement. One problem with such devices, including manually operated switches and push buttons, can cause signals to be misread. This phenomenon is known as "contact bounce" and is demonstrated in Fig. 4.9. A mechanical contact does not close cleanly; the metal contacts rebound at least once. This effect is normally more pronounced when the contact is opened. The bounce time varies with the design and size of the switch; a heavy-duty relay contact can bounce for up to 50 msec. This

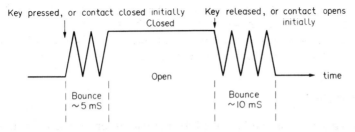

FIG. 4.9. Contact bounce.

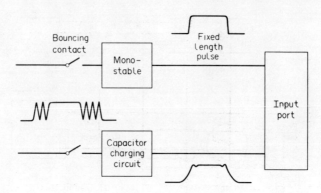

FIG. 4.10. Hardware solutions to cure contact bounce.

effect can cause the microcomputer to think that the contact has changed state more than once.

There are two solutions to this problem—hardware and software. The hardware solution involves inserting debounce circuitry. An example is shown in Fig. 4.10—two techniques are demonstrated. A monostable multivibrator generates a fixed length pulse when it is triggered by the first closure. Alternatively a capacitor charging circuit can be used to "smooth out" the unwanted pulses. However, this hardware solution is seldom used because it involves additional circuitry. It is far easier to remove the effects of bounce by software. When the software detects the first change in state of a contact, it should then not attempt to read a second change for typically 100 msec or more. Normally microcomputer software "scans" all, or a group, of its digital inputs on a regular basis. If this scanning speed is one scan every 100 msec, or slower, then contact bounce is overcome. However if the scanning speed is too slow, e.g. every 1 sec, legitimate signals from pushbutton operations may be missed. An optimum speed for keyboard scanning is one scan every 50 msec or 100 msec.

Recent solid-state transducers, which conveniently supply voltage levels, are infrared detectors and light-beam detectors, which indicate the presence of objects or movement. However, even these devices frequently use buffering electrical relays or optoisolators to provide electrical isolation between remote circuitry and the microcomputer.

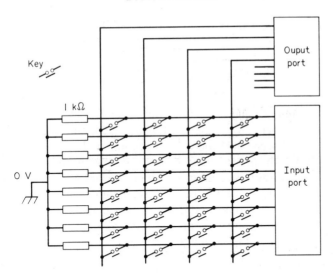

FIG. 4.11. Keyboard connection to a microcomputer.

The most common application of pushbutton inputs is a manual keyboard of course, and a special method of interconnecting a large array of keyboard signals is generally applied, as shown in Fig. 4.11. 32 keys are connected in this example. Four inputs ports could be utilised to perform the interface (together with 32 resistors), but a better method is applied as shown. Only $1\frac{1}{2}$ ports are required—an input port and one-half of an output port. The 32 keys are arranged in a matrix of 4 columns and 8 rows. If the top output signal is set to 1, then a combination of 8 1s and 0s are presented on the input port. These 8 bits represent the state of the left-hand column of keys—a closed contact, i.e. pushbutton depressed, sets a 1. Therefore, although there is a saving in hardware ($2\frac{1}{2}$ ports and 24 resistors) there is an additional requirement in software, which must scan each of the four columns of keys in succession. Each of the four stages consists of the following software functions:

(i) Output one bit to select a column of keys.
(ii) Input all eight bits.
(iii) Examine the bits, and if any is set to 1 jump to a program section

which services the key entry, e.g. echo key character back to a display.
 (iv) Delay (typically 100 msec).
 (v) Repeat (total of four times).

Stage (ii) is often termed "strobing in" the key settings. The keyboard connections are made in a "matrix" arrangement.

One additional circuit arrangement, which is commonly applied when a keyboard and segment display are combined within the same micro-computer, is worthy of examination. The system is shown in Fig. 4.12. If the reader compares this diagram with Figs. 4.6 and 4.11 he will identify the standard methods of both driving a segment display and scanning a keyboard. The decoded 10 output digit lines perform two completely separate functions. Firstly, they are used to select a display digit which is to receive the segment pattern a to p during the display drive program. Secondly, they are used when a column of keys is read during the keyboard scan program. Notice that problems can arise during the keyboard scan program, when a column of keys is strobed, but simultaneously a display digit is selected. Therefore, the segment pattern, which was latched on the segment lines previously, could inadvertently appear on the selected display unit. For this reason a single output bit (display select) is used to gate the segment pattern through to the display module only when the display program runs.

This "multiplexed", i.e. different signal types share the same lines, arrangement enables less than three ports (19 signals) to handle a total of 140 separate signals (80 segments plus 60 keys).

Notice that the matrixing arrangement, which is used generally with keyboards, can also be applied with remote contact closures. Some industrial logging microcomputers can handle up to 512 contact closure inputs. The simple circuit of Fig. 4.13 uses only $1\frac{1}{2}$ ports to scan 128 plant contact closures. The only difference between this arrangement and the circuit which is used for a keyboard is that a "blocking diode" is placed in series with every contact. This feature is required because, unlike a keyboard, large numbers of contacts in this matrix may be closed simultaneously; in a keyboard only one key is pressed at any time. If the diodes are not used, and contacts CC1, CC121 and CC128 are all closed together with CC8 open, then when the CC1 to CC8 column is strobed with a 1, a current path exists from the strobed line through CC1, CC121 and CC128

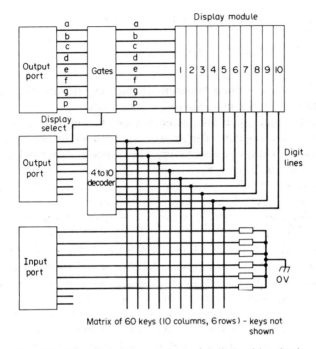

FIG. 4.12. Combined keyboard and segment display drive circuit.

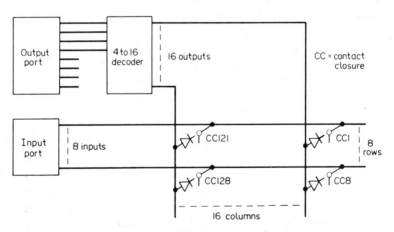

FIG. 4.13. Matrix of 128 plant contact closures.

to incorrectly set a 1 on the bottom input line. The blocking diodes prevent this path.

The advantages of this arrangement are:

(a) $1\frac{1}{2}$ ports are required in place of 16 ports.
(b) Considerable cabling costs can be saved if the contacts are some distance from the microcomputer. For example, only 24 (16 output + 8 input) signals or cable cores are required to connect to the remote assembly of contact closures, compared with 256 (2 cable cores for each contact closure) if matrixing is not applied. The matrixing interconnection system can be arranged from a remote terminal strip to the plant contacts.

The disadvantage of this system is that 128 diodes are required. However, these diodes can be readily wired across the remote terminal strip, and their cost is far outweighed by the saving in cable cost.

(Notice that digital outputs can be multiplexed in the same way as digital inputs. However this is rarely implemented for security reasons. Consider the sharing, or multiplexing, of a single output port between a group of eight relays and another group of eight LEDs. If a failure in the multiplexing circuit occurs, the settings for the LEDs may be incorrectly output to the relays. If the relays are performing vital plant control functions, e.g. start a conveyor or close an isolator valve, the consequences could be disastrous).

BIBLIOGRAPHY

1. *Microprocessor Interfacing Techniques*. Rodnay Zaks and Austin Lesea. Sybex, 1981.

CHAPTER 5

Analogue Interfacing Techniques

5.1 ANALOGUE TRANSDUCERS

An analogue reading is one which is continuous, i.e. it can take any value over its range. Analogue signals are generally monitored from a plant by microcomputers in order to measure plant parameters such as temperature, flow, pressure, level, weight, speed, chemical analysis, etc. In this section we will examine the actual plant transducer which generates an electrical signal, and in the next section we will investigate the amplification and conversion circuits which interpose this signal and the microcomputer input port.

(a) Temperature Transducers

Figure 5.1 illustrates three common transducers for temperature measurement. The thermocouple is a welded junction of dissimilar metals (e.g. iron and constantan, or chromel and alumel), which generates a small voltage (e.g. up to 50 mV) when it is heated. It is an extremely accurate device and specialised types can measure very high temperatures. Its disadvantages are that its response is non-linear and also it is necessary to use expensive "compensating cable" for signal transmission if accuracy is to be retained. Also a temperature-stabilised "cold junction" (normally at 0°C) should be maintained at some point in the circuit.

The resistance thermometer, or "thermistor", is a simple device which generates a variable resistance when the temperature rises. Commonly it

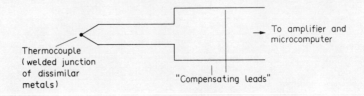

(a) Thermocouple

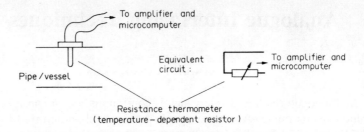

(b) Resistance thermometer ("thermistor")

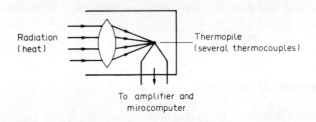

(c) Radiation pyrometer

FIG. 5.1. Temperature transducers.

is made from a winding of nickel wire, and it is applied widely for low temperature ranges (up to 300°C).

The radiation pyrometer is a non-contact device which can be used to measure extremely high temperatures. It captures radiant energy and generates a relatively large electrical signal using a thermocouple assembly.

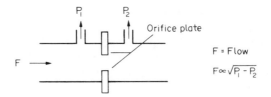

(a) Orifice plate (differential pressure measurement)

F = Flow

$F \propto \sqrt{P_1 - P_2}$

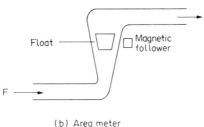

(b) Area meter

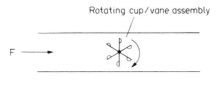

(c) Anemometer

FIG. 5.2. Flow transducers.

(b) Flow Transducers

Figure 5.2 shows the method of operation of three common flow transducers. The orifice plate is the most common of a range of "differential pressure" flow transducers. The principle of operation is that an obstruction, e.g. an orifice plate, causes a pressure drop in a gas or liquid flow, and this pressure drop is related to flow. The flow reading is highly non-linear (square root of differential pressure), produces a pressure drop and gives poor accuracy (typically 2% to 5%). However, it is a cheap and reliable technique.

In the area meter the vertical position of a float, which is suspended in a gas or liquid flow, is used as a measure of the flow rate. Signal generation is achieved by the use of an external magnetic follower or by mechanical linkage to the float stem.

The speed of rotation of the cup or vane assembly is taken as a measurement of flow in an anemometer.

(c) Pressure Transducers

Figure 5.3 shows three pressure transducers. The Bourdon tube is a

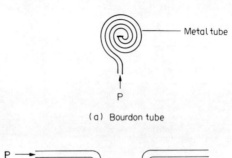

(a) Bourdon tube

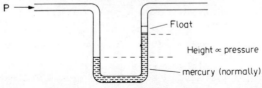

(b) Manometer (U–tube)

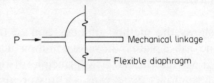

(c) Diaphragm

Fig. 5.3. Pressure transducers.

twisted metal tube which deforms when pressure is applied. The movement of the free end is mechanically linked to a device which generates an electrical signal (commonly a DVT—differential voltage transformer; this is described later in section 5.2).

In the manometer a column of mercury is displaced by pressure changes. A mechanism is added, e.g. a float, to provide external movement which can be converted to an electrical signal.

The operation of a diaphragm is straightforward. A bellows assembly is a more complicated variation of the same principle.

(d) Level Transducers

Figure 5.4 shows the principle of operation of three level transducers.

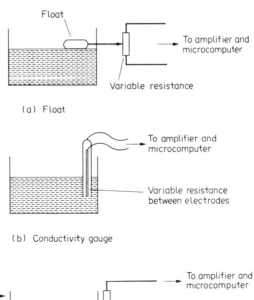

(a) Float

(b) Conductivity gauge

(c) Gamma radiation

Fig. 5.4. Level transducers.

The float operated device, which drives an external variable resistor, is the same technique which is used for level measurement of petrol in cars.

The conductivity gauge is useful for large variations in level. The conductivity between the two electrodes increases as level increases.

The absorption of gamma radiation by the liquid in the vessel varies the amount of radiation which reaches the detector in the radiation transducer.

(e) Weight Transducers

The two common devices which are used to measure weight are shown in Fig. 5.5. When an electrical resistance strain gauge or a semiconductor strain gauge is mounted in the load-bearing assembly, a variable electrical resistance is generated when a weight is applied. The latter device gives a bigger resistance change, but it is less accurate and more temperature sensitive.

An assembly of strain gauges is sometimes termed a "load cell".

Other transducers can be used for these same types of measurement. Additionally transducers are available to measure speed, thickness, gas analysis, pH factor, humidity, etc.

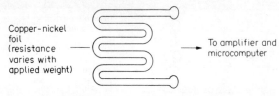

Copper-nickel foil (resistance varies with applied weight)

To amplifier and microcomputer

(a) Electrical resistance strain gauge

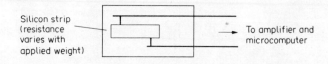

Silicon strip (resistance varies with applied weight)

To amplifier and microcomputer

(b) Semiconductor strain gauge

FIG. 5.5. Weight transducers.

5.2 ANALOGUE INPUT CIRCUITS

Various signal processing techniques are needed to manipulate each of the following three common types of transducer signal before they can be presented to a microcomputer: variable voltage (e.g. thermocouple), variable resistance (e.g. conductivity gauge, and many others) and mechanical movement (e.g. Bourdon tube movement). Descriptions of these techniques follow.

(a) Variable Voltage

The standard amplifier which is used as an instrumentation amplifier is an "operational amplifier", or op-amp. This possesses slightly different characteristics to an amplifier which amplifies telephone, radio or television signals. It must amplify at an extremely low frequency, in fact it must amplify signals which are slow moving and even can be at a steady DC level. Special circuit techniques are used to produce this feature, viz. the use of balanced pairs of transistors, and this leads to the characteristics of high temperature stability and excellent common mode noise rejection. This latter feature involves the rejection of an unwanted voltage on each of the two conductors which connect to the device; this phenomenon is common in instrumentation systems.

Op-amps are now produced in integrated circuit form. The circuit arrangement for voltage signal amplification using an op-amp is shown in Fig. 5.6. The voltage gain for this arrangement is:

$$-\frac{R_2}{R_1} \quad \text{(typically 100)}.$$

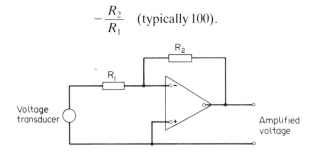

Fig. 5.6. Op-amp circuit (inverting).

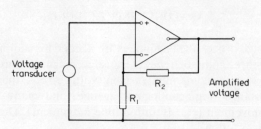

FIG. 5.7. Op-amp circuit (non-inverting).

The minus sign shows that the amplifier inverts the input voltage. Also the input impedance is equal to R_1 (typically 10 kΩ). If a higher input impedance is required so that less circuit loading is placed on the preceding transducer circuit, or alternatively if a non-inverting gain is required, the circuit of Fig. 5.7 is applied.

The most common op-amp IC is the 741, which can be purchased for less than £1. FET (field effect transistor) op-amp ICs are available and these can offer an extremely high input impedance, which is an attractive feature with some transducers, e.g. optical devices.

More sophisticated circuits based on the op-amp can perform a linearising function as well as amplification.

(b) Variable Resistance

Most transducers are of the variable resistance type, e.g. resistance thermometer, conductivity gauge and strain gauge, and a "bridge" circuit must precede an op-amp, as shown in Fig. 5.8. In the Wheatstone bridge four resistors of the same value form the four arms of the bridge and present a state of balance in the bridge. One of the resistors is the transducer, which is installed at the appropriate measuring point in the pipe/vessel. When this resistance value varies, an imbalance signal is generated in the bridge, and this signal is amplified by the op-amp.

Clearly conventional resistors of 5% or 10% accuracy should not be used for the three fixed resistors in the bridge. Precision components should be applied.

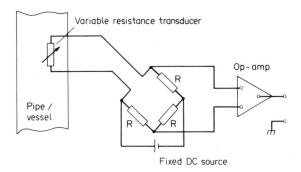

FIG. 5.8. Use of Wheatstone bridge for variable resistance transducer.

(c) Mechanical Movement

A range of circuit techniques are used to convert from mechanical movement to an electrical signal. Figure 5.9 shows the principle of operation of a DVT (differential voltage transformer), which is commonly applied. Mechanical movement from the transducer, e.g. Bourdon tube, float, diaphragm, adjusts the position of the former, which in turn alters the magnetic coupling between the primary winding and the two secondary windings. Therefore the relative magnitudes of the output voltages E_1 and E_2 varies. The voltage difference $(E_1 - E_2)$ is rectified and amplified.

Alternatively, a variable inductance in a coil can be introduced by movement of a magnetic former, which is adjacent to the coil, as shown

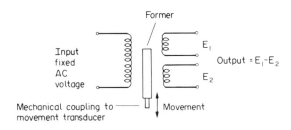

FIG. 5.9. Differential voltage transformer.

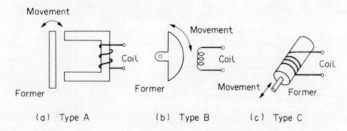

FIG. 5.10. Variable inductance (movement to electrical signal converter).

in Fig. 5.10. The variable capacitance equivalent is shown in Fig. 5.11. In each of these cases the variable inductor/capacitor forms part of an AC bridge. Imbalance in the bridge causes a phase sensitive detector to generate a DC signal which can be amplified and presented to the microcomputer as shown in Fig. 5.12. Alternatively the inductor/capacitor may form part of a tuned circuit oscillator, and the variable frequency generated is followed by a frequency to DC converter.

We are now in a position to draw the full circuit connections for most analogue input systems through from transducer to A/D (analogue to digital) converter. Figure 5.13 shows a simplified arrangement for a weight measurement. The A/D converter is an IC which possesses a high input impedance. The op-amp circuit presents to it a signal which can have one of the following typical ranges:

(a) 0 to 10 V,
(b) 4 to 20 mA,
    and others.

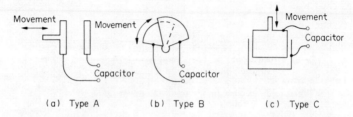

FIG. 5.11. Variable capacitance (movement to electrical signal converter).

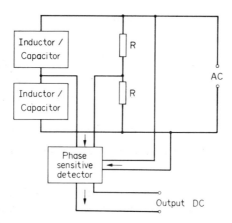

FIG. 5.12. Inductor or capacitor bridge.

The essential difference to emphasise is that these ranges are expressed as voltage or current ranges. Voltage signals are easier to handle and to understand. However current ranges are used frequently in industry. A current signal is generated in the op-amp circuit such that the same current signal is produced for a particular transducer input signal reading, regardless (within reason) of the circuit resistance which is connected to the output signal. This gives the advantage that long cable lengths, with increased cable resistance and consequent voltage drop along the cable, do not cause erroneous voltage signals to be presented to the A/D. The same voltage is presented to the A/D across the terminating resistor R, because the current is held constant, regardless of cable length. R is much lower than the input resistance of the A/D and so the current range of 4 to

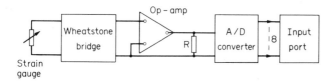

FIG. 5.13. Input circuit for weight measurement.

20 mA across 500 Ω presents the following voltage to the A/D converter:

$$V = I \times R = (4 \text{ to } 20 \text{ mA}) \times 500 \text{ Ω} = 2 \text{ to } 10 \text{ V}.$$

Notice that a "live zero" of 4 mA (which equates to 2 V in this case) exists. This is a useful feature because it indicates that even if the transducer is reading zero, representing no flow-rate for example, then an active electrical signal is present. This is different from the fault condition of 0 mA, which exists if a wire breaks or the op-amp circuit fails or is switched off, etc. In a voltage range system the maintenance technician cannot distinguish between a faulty circuit and a valid zero reading if 0 V is present.

The A/D chip itself can be one of two basic types: successive approximation or integrating (or dual-ramp). The former gives an extremely fast conversion time—typically 20 μsec. The latter is slow (50 msec), but it is more immune to electrical noise and drift. Details of internal operation of such devices can be found in many standard textbooks. It is only necessary here to note a typical method of connection for such a device, as shown in Fig. 5.14 for a successive approximation A/D converter. A single analogue input signal is converted into an 8-bit digital value. Clock pulses, e.g. 600 kHz, must be injected to time the conversion process, and also a start conversion trigger pulse must be connected to initiate a conversion (this could be an output port connection from the microcomputer). A conversion complete signal is generated by the device, and this can be connected if required to an input port so that software can ignore a reading unless conversion is finished. This particular IC gives an 8-bit

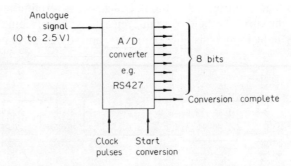

FIG. 5.14. A/D converter (successive approximation type).

reading, but more accurate 10-bit and 12-bit devices are available; two ports are then required in the microcomputer to handle the count. The price of A/Ds is dependent on the conversion rate and the resolution that is required.

If an input signal fluctuates rapidly, it is sometimes necessary to insert a "sample-and-hold" circuit before the A/D. This is simply an op-amp which has a large capacitor connected across its input.

Although A/D chips are relatively cheap (a few pounds only), it is often cost-effective in a large analogue input system to share one device amongst several input readings. A typical method of "multiplexing" several analogue values is demonstrated in Fig. 5.15. A 4-bit code is output by software to a multiplexor chip in order to select one input analogue signal, which is passed through to the A/D converter and input port. Therefore the drive program within the microcomputer must select each reading in turn, generate a delay (to allow time for the multiplexor to settle and for the A/D converter to generate the digital value) and then repeat the process, until all analogue readings are scanned. This system saves the cost of 15 A/D chips and 15 associated input ports (more if A/D is 10- or 12-bit). However, one output port and a multiplexor IC are required, and the security of the input system is diminished—if the A/D chip fails then all 16 input readings are lost.

It is necessary to mention one final device, which is required for pneumatic transducers. Traditionally a large proportion of instrumentation and transducer systems in industry are pneumatic (air-operated). If such a pneumatic transducer is to be interfaced to a microcomputer, then

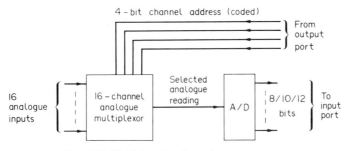

FIG. 5.15. Multiplexed analogue input system.

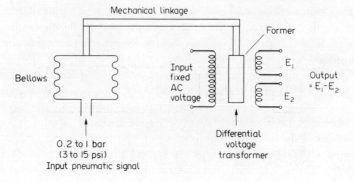

FIG. 5.16. P-E (pneumatic to electric) converter.

a P-E (pneumatic to electric) converter is required, as shown in Fig. 5.16. The device is based on the DVT, which was described earlier.

5.3 ANALOGUE OUTPUT CIRCUITS

Analogue output signals are not as common as analogue input signals. The latter are often applied in large numbers when microcomputers collect data from industrial plant. However, the requirement for microcomputers to generate analogue signals is limited generally to the following areas:

(a) desired position to a servo,
(b) setpoint to a three-term controller.

Servos (motor-driven position control systems) are used in peripheral devices such as graph plotters or pen recorders. Also servos find application in robots and equipment such as aerial-positioning, gun-positioning, etc. The method of connection to a servo, and the basic diagram of a servo, are demonstrated in Fig. 5.17. The output port feeds a D/A (digital to analogue) converter (8-bit device shown), which generates an analogue value. This value represents the desired position to the servo. The servo consists of a subtractor circuit (desired position—actual position), which generates an error signal when the controlled shaft is not at the required position. This error signal causes a motor to rotate until the error is zero.

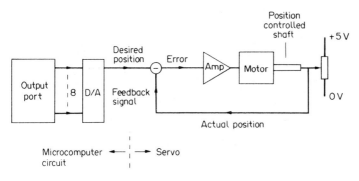

FIG. 5.17. Microcomputer-driven servo for position control.

This arrangement is used to drive an inking pen in a chart recorder, or to drive each of the X and Y deflection mechanisms in a plotter. Five or six such circuits are required in an industrial robot for the five or six degrees of freedom; a servo-driven robot, although more expensive, gives much more precise position control than a stepper motor robot. Some electrical actuating valves, which form part of process control systems, are servo driven, and therefore a microcomputer drive uses this same system.

A non-servo application is the connection of a microcomputer setpoint to a three-term controller, as shown in Fig. 5.18. The feedback system

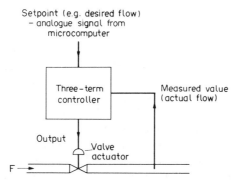

FIG. 5.18. Three-term controller with microcomputer-generated setpoint.

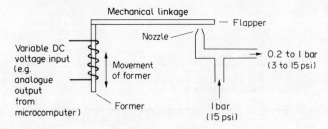

FIG. 5.19. E-P (electric to pneumatic) converter.

within the controller, which is based on the measured value signal, is identical in principle to the operation of a servo. The separate three-term controller is a standard item of equipment in industrial processes, and nowadays is itself microcomputer-based.

The D/A chip itself is normally based on the "resistor ladder" principle, and again is well documented in standard textbooks. 8, 10 and 12 bit devices are available. The circuit connection to an output port is much more straightforward than for an A/D converter and its associated connection to an input port. No clock or any additional signal connection is required, e.g. 8 input digital signal lines and one output analogue signal line are the only connections, as shown in Fig. 5.17.

Multiplexing is not performed normally with analogue output signals for the same reason that applies for digital outputs, i.e. system security. A failure in a complete group of important control signals can result from a fault in the multiplexing circuit.

If an analogue output feeds a pneumatic instrumentation system then an E-P (electric to pneumatic) converter is required. Figure 5.19 shows a typical principle of operation. An analogue output signal varies the current in the electric winding. This causes the former to move vertically. Mechanical coupling to a "flapper" beam causes variable throttling of a nozzle. This in turn varies the pneumatic signal delivered at the output.

BIBLIOGRAPHY

1. *Microcomputers for Process Control*. R. C. Holland. Pergamon, 1983.
2. *Design of Op-amp Circuits, With Experiments*. Howard M. Berlin. Prentice-Hall, 1977.

CHAPTER 6

Special Peripheral Interfacing

6.1 FLOPPY DISK

A bulk storage peripheral device is required in many microcomputer systems so that a large number of programs and data files can be held. These programs are then loaded down into system memory (RAM) when they are required to run.

There are two common devices which perform this function: the hard disk and the floppy disk. A hard disk gives very large storage capacity— typically 10 Mbytes (10 million bytes)—and is fast in terms of data access and data transfer. It is often known by the name of the dominant manufacturer, i.e. Winchester. The disadvantage of a hard disk is that it is expensive—typically five times more expensive than a floppy disk.

Floppy disk drive units are far more common. Apart from the price advantage, they offer the feature of removable disks, i.e. the recording surface unit (simply called "disk" or "diskette") can be removed from the drive and replaced by a different unit which holds a different set of programs. The storage capacity of a floppy disk can range from 100 Kbytes (100 thousand bytes) to over 500 Kbytes.

There are two standard sizes for floppy disks, as shown in Fig. 6.1. The same features apply to both 8 inch and $5\frac{1}{4}$ inch disks, as follows.

The flexible plastic disk, which is coated with a magnetic recording surface, is sealed within a paper envelope, and when inserted into the drive unit, rotates inside this envelope. A window is cut out of this envelope so that the read/write head can access the recording surface; in fact the heads actually touch the surface when data transfers occur—this

73

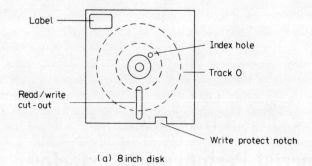

(a) 8 inch disk

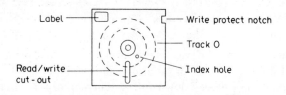

(b) 5¼ inch disk

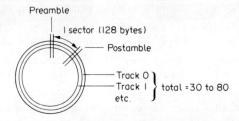

(c) Layout of data recording surface

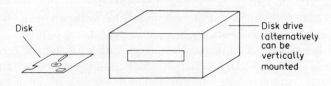

(d) Typical disk drive

FIG. 6.1. Floppy disk.

is called the "head load" action. A small circular hole is cut into the envelope. This is called the "index" hole, and an opto-detector senses this hole and generates a signal every revolution so that the control circuit can track the rotary motion of the disk. A write protect cut-out notch is set into the periphery of the paper envelope. This is used to prevent write operations to a disk which is designated to be read-only, e.g. it contains important programs or files which must not be overwritten. This notch must be uncovered to prevent write operations with an 8 inch disk, but covered to perform the function with a $5\frac{1}{4}$ inch disk. Disks can be single-sided or double-sided and single-density or double-density. The recording surface is divided into typically 30 to 80 tracks, and each track consists of several sectors. A sector is normally 128 bytes. Between each sector some sector identifying data is stored, e.g. the "self-address" in terms of track number and sector number. This address is checked by the control circuit when sectors are accessed in order to detect corruption or misalignment. The process of writing these addresses on a blank disk initially is called "initialising" or "formatting" the disk. The format invariably used is the IBM 3740 format, which is an industry standard.

The interfacing circuitry is relatively straightforward. Manufacturers of microprocessors frequently offer a floppy disk control chip to support their CPU, such is the wide application of floppy disks. Again a standard interface is used between this single control chip and the drive unit, which may be of Shughart or DR manufacture. A typical floppy disk controller IC is shown in Fig. 6.2. Software sends the chip the required track and

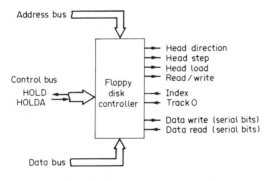

FIG. 6.2. Floppy disk controller IC.

sector address. The chip sets the Head Direction and the Head Step signals appropriately in order to move the read/write head to the required track. The chip uses the Index pulse to help it monitor the angular position (i.e. sector) of the disk. When it detects that the head is positioned at the start of the required track and sector, it sets the Head Load signal, which places the read/write head in contact with the disk surface. The Read/Write signal determines the direction of data transfer. Clearly data is written to and read from disk one-bit at a time, i.e. in serial form, on the Data Write and Data Read lines. Therefore the controller chip groups these bits into bytes to perform serial to parallel (for read) and parallel to serial (for write) conversion. The Track 0 signal is a reference signal to reset the chip's track counter at switch-on when the head is moved to the outer track.

A powerful feature which is commonly applied with data transfer between microcomputer and disk is DMA (direct memory access). In this system the transfer of a sector, or group of sectors, is initiated by software but the hardware, in the form of the floppy disk controller IC, then takes over the data transfer task. It transfers automatically byte-by-byte, without any further software involvement, between memory and disk.

Figure 6.3 shows the principle of operation of a DMA floppy disk controller IC. Software sends the IC the start address in memory of a data block which is used for DMA transfer, and it also sends the start address on disk (track and sector number) plus the number of sectors. The controller IC then takes over the transfer function. When it locates the

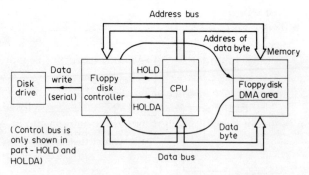

FIG. 6.3. DMA floppy disk controller (write operation).

required disk track and sector it generates a HOLD signal to the CPU. After obeying the current instruction the CPU responds with a HOLDA (HOLD acknowledge)—Fig. 6.2 also shows these signals. The controller then assumes control of the address bus and the data bus, and transfers data bytes directly between memory (invariably RAM of course) and disk without passing through the CPU. In some microprocessors the HOLD operation may not delay normal CPU operation if DMA transfers occur during "dead-time" on the buses, e.g. at certain stages in the fetch/execute cycle for each instruction the address and data buses are not actually in use.

DMA greatly eases software control of disks since discrete input or output commands do not have to be implemented for each byte transfer.

6.2 KEYBOARD ENCODER

In Chapter 4 we encountered the matrixing arrangement of a set of keyswitches in a keyboard. The application of both an output port (to "strobe" a block of keys) and an input port (to read in the settings of the selected keys) was described. Such arrangements are common, but they require that the drive software must perform a regular scan of the keyboard, e.g. 10 times per second, in order to avoid missing the manual operation of one of the keys.

Once again, as with the DMA floppy disk controller IC, hardware designers have developed a specialised input/output IC which saves the programmer a lot of work. A keyboard encoder chip can be used for a variety of keyboard matrix sizes, as shown in Fig. 6.4. In this arrangement the device performs a continuous automatic scan of a matrix of 64 keys. This scan is generated internally by hardware, and if a key is depressed a code is presented to the CPU's data bus. The most useful way of signalling to the CPU that a code is available to be read is by means of an interrupt signal. Therefore when the encoder IC detects that a key is closed, it can generate an interrupt signal, which causes the program that is running currently within the CPU to be suspended. A special interrupt program is then called in order to read the code, which identifies the key, from the encoder chip.

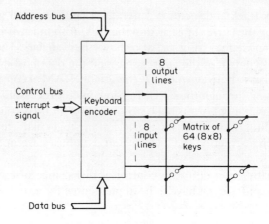

FIG. 6.4. Keyboard encoder.

6.3 CRT (CATHODE RAY TUBE)

Undoubtedly the CRT (cathode ray tube), in its form as an integrated display within a microcomputer box assembly or as a remote VDU (visual display unit), is the most ubiquitous device for passing information to an operator. The display can be a simple text display, e.g. a written message, or it can be a sophisticated colour graphics format, e.g. a histogram of company sales figures.

The normal method of generating a signal which feeds to a CRT from a microcomputer is demonstrated in Fig. 6.5. The scanning technique for a CRT involves deflection coils driving the electron beam across the screen in a series of several hundred horizontal lines in each picture or frame. Each frame is updated several times a second to avoid flicker. The drive circuitry modulates the beam in intensity to produce characters as a series of dots in order to construct a character. Figure 6.5 shows how the top two of the seven horizontal line scans contribute to the display of the letter "S". This technique is called "raster scan" video generation.

This system is demonstrated in a straightforward VDU terminal, which is shown in Fig. 6.6. The terminal displays typically 20 rows of characters, with 80 characters in each row. The characters which are required to be displayed are transmitted from the microcomputer by RS 232-C link and

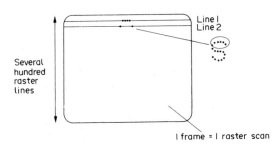

(a) Raster scan (not to scale)

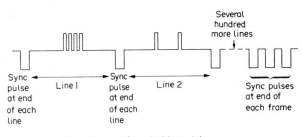

(b) Video waveform (not to scale)

FIG. 6.5. Video waveform for raster scan.

stored in internal RAM within the VDU. A character look-up ROM contains the bit patterns for typically a 5 by 7 dot matrix for each character type (e.g. letters, numbers); at 5 bytes per character, 320 ROM bytes are needed for 64 different characters. A video generator circuit samples the characters in RAM and uses the matrix pattern in ROM to generate the video waveform.

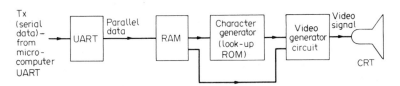

FIG. 6.6. Video generation using character look-up in VDU.

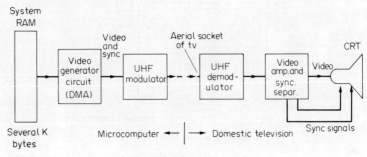

(a) Unmodified television receiver

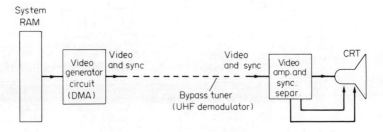

(b) Video monitor (or modified television receiver)

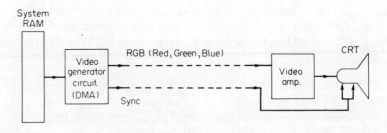

(c) RGB monitor

FIG. 6.7. Three types of TV monitor.

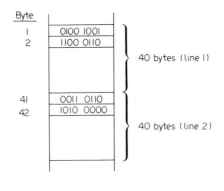

(a) Memory

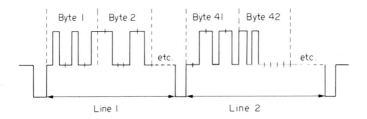

(b) Video waveform

FIG. 6.8. Memory mapped video.

A similar method is applied for direct microcomputer control of a display terminal. There are three basic methods as shown in Fig. 6.7, and the systems give increasing picture quality. The final system—the RGB monitor—is a colour monitor which can produce high quality and high resolution displays. DMA (direct memory access) is used by the video generator circuit to convert memory bytes into video signals. Therefore an area of main microcomputer memory must be reserved to hold this picture information.

Assume that in a non-graphics, i.e. text-only, system the screen format is arranged on a 24-line, 40 characters per line, basis. Figure 6.8 shows how the memory bit pattern is sampled by DMA to generate the corresponding video waveform. This arrangement is called "memory mapped video", and therefore large areas of memory (typically 8 K) must be reserved for generating the video signal. Software is used to pack this memory area with the required bytes.

If colour graphics are used in place of text-only displays, then individual screen dots, or "pixels", can be represented in RAM in the same manner, but additional bits must be used to specify colour. If 3 bits, in the form of a colour code, represent the colour of a pixel or group of pixels (to save memory space), then 8 colours can be represented. Several micro-computers, e.g. the Apple II and the Cromemco, offer text mode, low resolution graphics and high resolution graphics in one system, and software is used to select the display mode which is required.

Most CP/M (the most common master operating program) systems do not offer graphics, but several manufacturers offer an add-on board which provides high resolution monochrome or colour graphics facilities.

The disadvantages of raster-scan graphics are that a large area of system memory must be set aside to hold the picture information, and that complicated software is required to change a section of a graphics picture since data bytes are scattered throughout the display memory area.

Both Texas Instruments and Atari have helped to alleviate these problems by offering an "intelligent" CRT controller chip which allows the programmer to specify a display shape (called a "sprite") and to request a change in the position of that shape on the CRT by a selection of simple output commands. For example, two data output instructions to the Texas Instruments TMS 9918A cause a pre-defined shape, e.g. a blue aeroplane, to be shifted to a new position on the CRT. Overlapping sprites are allowed so that fast and complex animation is possible.

6.4 AUDIO CASSETTE RECORDER

An international standard signal specification exists for storing prog-rams and data files from microcomputers to audio cassette recorders. This is the Kansas standard or CUTS (Computer Users Tape System), which stores a logic 1 as a burst of sinewaves of one frequency and a logic 0 as a burst of sinewaves of a different frequency. Figure 6.9 shows the waveform of a data byte. It is recorded at a speed of 300 baud, and a logic 1 is represented by 8 sinewaves at 2400 Hz and a logic 0 is represented by

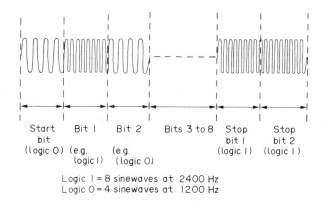

Logic 1 = 8 sinewaves at 2400 Hz
Logic 0 = 4 sinewaves at 1200 Hz

FIG. 6.9. Kansas standard—signal waveform for 1 byte.

4 sinewaves at 1200 Hz. A data byte is framed by a start bit (logic 0) and two stop bits (logic 1).

This waveform can be generated either by software or hardware. Software can pulse a single bit on a parallel output port at the frequencies required; the square wave produced is rounded and smoothed by the cassette recorder.

A hardware solution is to generate the bit pattern at 300 baud and to use a modem circuit to create the bursts of 2400 Hz and 1200 Hz sinewaves. A typical circuit is shown in Fig. 6.10. A clock pulse at 4800 Hz is divided in

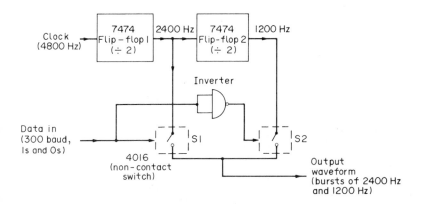

FIG. 6.10. Kansas standard modulator circuit.

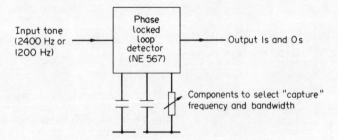

FIG. 6.11. Kansas standard demodulator circuit.

two flip-flops to 2400 Hz and 1200 Hz. Only one of these frequencies is gated out through one of the semiconductor switches S1 or S2 to the output connection, so that as the "data in" signal switches between 0 and 1, the output waveform carries bursts of 2400 Hz and 1200 Hz squarewaves. The signal in to the circuit could be pulsed at 300 baud by software, or it could be connected from the output of a UART, which is set to run at 300 baud.

Clearly the output of this circuit feeds the input signal connection to a cassette recorder. Additionally the recorder motor must be switched to run when data transfers occur. This could be performed manually, but it is better performed under automatic control from the microcomputer by means of an additional single-bit output. A transistor drive to an electrical relay is required (see Fig. 4.1) in order to provide contact closure for switching power to the motor.

The circuit arrangement for data transfer in the reverse direction (from cassette recorder to microcomputer) can be based on an extremely useful IC—the phase locked loop detector. This particular device generates either a 1 or a 0 at its output dependent on the frequency of the incoming waveform. Figure 6.11 shows how it is applied to demodulate the 2400 Hz and 1200 Hz sine/squarewaves from the cassette recorder into 1s and 0s. If the phase locked loop detector is set to detect 2400 Hz by means of external components, then a 1 is set at its output for an input tone of this frequency. At any other frequency, i.e. at 1200 Hz, a 0 is set at the output. This output signal can then be scanned by software using a single-bit parallel input bit, or it could feed a UART.

The technique of converting from a tone to a logic level, and vice versa, is often called FSK (Frequency Shift Keying).

6.5 SPEECH SYNTHESISER

Speech synthesis is the latest and most appealing technique which has been added to the array of microcomputer interfacing facilities. A small number of ICs generate the audio signals which are used to drive a loudspeaker. Words and sentences can be generated.

Several manufacturers produce a variety of speech synthesiser chips which operate in circuits which use a diverse range of techniques. Basically a single chip forms the main audio generator and control function, whilst memory chips (normally EPROM) provide the sound code. The two contrasting methods of speech generation are:

(a) generate only one sound, so that several sounds must be concatenated to produces a word,
(b) generate a complete word, e.g. ALARM, TEN, ENTER.

The former method is more flexible because an almost unlimited vocabulary can be constructed. However, words which are generated are often of poor clarity and intelligibility. For this reason the second method is more common, and a speech synthesiser circuit of this type may offer typically several hundred words.

A typical method of operation is shown in Fig. 6.12. Connection to the microcomputer is via the usual latched parallel ports, e.g. a PIO. Handshaking of control signals is required, e.g. the speech synthesiser circuit sets a busy signal whilst it is generating a word. The word required is selected by sending an EPROM address from an output port. This address is sent in two 8-bit halves, so that the EPROM addressing circuitry latches the two halves and selects a particular EPROM and an address on that EPROM. The selected memory bytes (perhaps 60 bytes) are then transferred from EPROM and converted into a serial bit pattern. The speech synthesiser chip uses this bit stream to create the required mixture of tones which simulate the speech word. A low frequency filter and amplifier process the audio signal between the speech synthesiser and the loudspeaker.

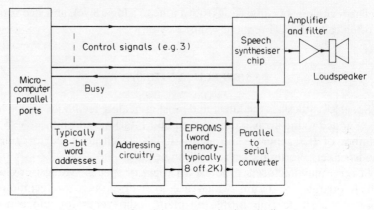

Complete speech synthesiser circuit

FIG. 6.12. Typical speech synthesiser (and microcomputer interface).

A variation of this arrangement is to replace the fixed EPROM word code bytes with main memory RAM within the microcomputer, so that the vocabulary of the system can be varied. A large amount of RAM is required, e.g. 100 words requires 8 Kbytes, and this can be updated from floppy disk.

Some personal computers, e.g. the ACT Sirius and the BBC microcomputer, offer a built-in facility for speech synthesis. Applications of a speech synthesiser circuit which is microcomputer driven are:

    (a) the British Leyland Maestro car,
    (b) spoken warning messages in industrial applications,
    (c) speech generation for disabled people,
    (d) games.

Examples of speech synthesiser chips are the Texas Instruments TMS 5100 and TMS 5200, General Instruments SP-0250, Triangle Digital Services TDS-90 and the Votrax SC-01A. Several firms offer a service which produces an EPROM-based vocabulary of words associated with a particular speech synthesiser chip. The service includes the facility for the customer to record his own message/sentence on EPROM. Further several firms offer a comprehensive "talking board", which is interfaced conveniently to any microcomputer. At least one such board possesses its own microprocessor to assist in the speech generation process, together with a parallel or serial interface to the separate driving microcomputer.

6.6 COMMON BUSES

A common bus is a standard set of interfacing connections which allows different microprocessors to interface with input/output boards from a range of different manufacturers. The specification of a universal common bus has not proved to be practicable, but two widely used common bus standards are used, as follows.

(a) S-100 Bus

The S-100 bus is the most widely used, and is often termed the IEEE 696. It consists of a list of 100 signal connections. These are arranged to occupy precise pin numbers on a double-row (50 + 50) edge connector, which inserts into a mating socket to feed along a back-plane to other S-100 boards. Figure 6.13 demonstrates the method of interconnection.

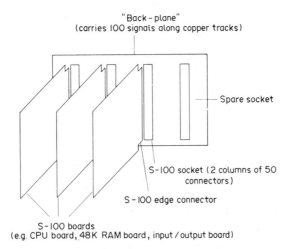

FIG. 6.13. Interconnection of S-100 boards.

1	+8V	51	+8V
2	+16V	52	-16V
3	XRDY	53	GND
4	VI0	54	SLAVE CLR
5	VI1	55	DMA0
6	VI2	56	DMA1
7	VI3	57	DMA2
8	VI4	58	sXTRQ
9	VI5	59	AI9
10	VI6	60	SIXTN
11	VI7	61	A20
12	NMI	62	A21
13	PWRFAIL	63	A22
14	DMA3	64	A23
15	AI8	65	NDEF
16	AI6	66	NDEF
17	AI7	67	PHANTOM
18	SDSB	68	MWRT
19	CDSB	69	RFU
20	GND	70	GND
21	NDEF	71	RFU
22	ADSB	72	RDY
23	DODSB	73	INT
24	φ	74	HOLD
25	pSTVAL	75	RESET
26	pHLDA	76	pSYNC
27	RFU	77	pWR
28	RFU	78	pDBIN
29	A5	79	A0
30	A4	80	A1
31	A3	81	A2
32	AI5	82	A6
33	AI2	83	A7
34	A9	84	A8
35	DOUT1	85	AI3
36	DOUT0	86	AI4
37	AI0	87	AI1
38	DOUT4	88	DOUT2
39	DOUT5	89	DOUT3
40	DOUT6	90	DOUT7
41	DIN2	91	DIN4
42	DIN3	92	DIN5
43	DIN7	93	DIN6
44	sM1	94	DIN1
45	sOUT	95	DIN0
46	sINP	96	sINTA
47	sMEMR	97	sWO
48	sHLTA	98	ERROR
49	CLOCK	99	POC
50	GND	100	GND

FIG. 6.14. S-100 signal identities.

Boards are either 5 inch or 10 inch deep (at right angles to the edge connector).

The S-100 bus was designed to handle 8080, 8085 and Z80 microprocessor systems. However, 6502 and 6800 systems can be adapted to fit the S-100 standard.

The signal identities are shown in Fig. 6.14. The power supply rail voltages are $+8$ V, $+16$ V and -16 V. Individual boards must possess their own DC regulators to reduce these voltage levels as required, e.g. to $+5$ V, $+12$ V and -12 V. The normal CPU bidirectional data bus is split into separate directional input and output bus systems. Clearly not all of the 100 interconnections are used in most systems. This feature can lead occasionally to variable and non-standard use of some of the lines, and can cause problems when interconnecting S-100 boards from different manufacturers.

The obvious advantage of the use of an S-100 microcomputer, or any common bus arrangement, is that additional boards can be inserted in spare sockets, e.g. to extend input/output facilities, add colour graphics, include a hard disk interface, etc.

(b) IEEE 488 Bus 𝒳

The IEEE 488 bus possesses only 24 lines as follows:

(1) 8 data lines (bi-directional),
(2) 8 control lines,
(3) 8 ground lines.

Clearly the 8 data lines are used to carry the CPU's data bus and two halves of the address bus. This means that boards which connect to this bus standard require more circuitry to process these three functions than an S-100 board.

The construction of an IEEE 488 system follows the same format as for an S-100 multi-board system (see Fig. 6.13) except that a 24-pin connector is used. The identities of the control signals are as follows:

Control of   DAV—data valid
data byte   NRFD—not ready for data
transfer   NDAC—no data accepted

                   IFC—interface clear
Bus   ATN—attention
control   SRQ—service request
signals   REN—remote enable
                   EOI—end or identify

The two most important control signals are DAV, which can be used to set tri-state latches when data is valid on the 8 data lines, and ATN, which identifies data or address on the data lines.

Each board, or "device" in an IEEE 488 system can operate in a talk, listen and control mode. The CPU board operates in all three modes, a memory board in the first two modes, an output board in only the listen mode, and an input board operates in only the talk mode.

The Commodore PET personal computer uses the IEEE 488 bus. Two different types of PIO—the 6520 PIA (for data lines) and the 6522 VIA (for control lines)—are used to generate the bus. The latter device is also used in the BBC computer and is described in more detail in section 11.2.

The IEEE 488 bus, which was developed originally by Hewlett-Packard, is often known as the GPIB (General Purpose Interface Bus). It is used frequently for interfacing to instrumentation via a D/A and A/D board.

One final bus standard must be mentioned here for completeness. This is the RS 232-C serial interface and it has been described previously (section 3.3). It is used for interfacing a microcomputer to a remote peripheral, e.g. printer, VDU or another computer. It is unlike the S-100 and IEEE 488 buses because it does not require a large number of interconnecting parallel signals and it is not used for interconnecting boards along a back-plane.

BIBLIOGRAPHY

1. *Microcomputer Interfacing*. B. Artwick. Prentice-Hall, London, 1980.
2. A Graphics Primer. Gregg Williams. *Byte*, November 1982.
3. Talking Technology. Mark Sheppard. *Practical Computing*, Vol. 6, Issue 6, June 1983.
4. *Microcomputers for Process Control*. R. C. Holland. Pergamon, 1983.
5. Personal Computers in Automation Systems. D. Pritty and D. Barrie. *Microprocessors and Microsystems*, Vol. 5, Number 4, 1981.
6. *The S-100 and Other Buses*. Elmer C. Poe and James C. Goodwin. Prentice-Hall, 1979.

CHAPTER 7

Programming Techniques

7.1 MACHINE CODE AND ASSEMBLY LANGUAGE

There are two broad levels of programming: low level and high level. High-level programming can be performed by any lucid layman and it does not require an understanding of machine operation. Low-level programming requires a good knowledge of microprocessor operation and machine architecture.

Within the classification of low-level programming there are two subdivisions: machine code and assembly language. These are described as follows:

(a) Machine Code

This involves writing a program in binary, or more conveniently in its hexadecimal equivalent. Instructions in both 8-bit and 16-bit microprocessors are frequently multiword, i.e. consist of 1, 2 or 3 words. Thus the "opcode" and "operand" frequently occupy different words, as the following three-instruction program example shows (H = hex.):

Memory Location

1400	3A	Opcode	} LDA 1065H
1401	65	} Operand	
1402	10		
1403	3D	Opcode	DCR A
1404	C6	Opcode	} ADI 7
1405	07	Operand	

It is assumed that this short section of program is held in memory starting at location hex. 1400. It is written in 8-bit Intel 8080, 8085 and Zilog Z80 machine code—they are compatible. The program demonstrates the three different length instructions (2, 1 and 3 byte respectively).

The function of the program section is:

Memory address	Machine code	Mnemonic	Comments
1400	3A,65,10	LDA 1065H	Load accumulator with contents of address hex. 1065
1403	3D	DCR A	Decrement (subtract 1 from) accumulator
1404	C6,07	ADI 7	Add (immediate) 7 to accumulator

The program transfers the contents of memory location hex. 1065 into the accumulator, decrements it and then adds 7 to it.

A machine code programmer therefore requires the following knowledge before he can enter a program:

(1) An understanding of CPU operation, e.g. identities of accumulator and other work registers, a memory map, e.g. areas of ROM and RAM, and input/output addresses.

(2) A list of the instruction set for the particular microprocessor which he is programming.

(3) The ability to write his program in mnemonic form, i.e. use meaningful characters for each instruction (e.g. LDA, DCR and ADI).

(4) The equivalent machine code for each instruction, so that he can transpose his program into a binary/hexadecimal multi-byte version.

He then requires a program which already exists within the microcomputer, e.g. normally ROM-resident and called the "monitor" program, to allow him to enter his program directly into memory (RAM obviously).

Machine code programming is laborious and is fraught with error possibilities, particularly in (4) above, when an instruction of perhaps 3 bytes is converted into hexadecimal form. It is only applied if programming in any other form is not possible, e.g. in a small microcomputer training board. It is far easier to perform low-level programming in assembly language, as is described next.

(b) Assembly Language

In this process the program instructions are entered into the machine in mnemonic form. Therefore a program, which has a similar role to the monitor program for machine code, already exists in the microcomputer in order to convert the mnemonic instructions into machine code and insert them into memory. The program is called an "assembler". The two primary advantages of assembly language programming are that the programmer needs only use mnemonics for instructions (he can forget hex. opcodes) and that he can use labels for memory addresses. A label is any group of characters, e.g. CHARLIE, which he can give to a specific memory location. If he uses that location at any point in his program, then he simply refers to it by name (CHARLIE). Thus he can forget absolute memory addresses of program instructions and data items. Therefore, in the machine code program example given above, he does not need to calculate and record the first two columns of hex. numbers.

Consider the following program, which is written in Intel 8080/8085 assembly language (a complete list of Intel instructions is given later in section 8.1):

```
MVI  A,100     ; Load A (accumulator) with 100
MVI  B,50      ; Load B with 50
ADD  A,B       ; Add B to A (answer in A)
STA  2000H     ; Store A in memory location hex. 2000
```

The programmer gains entry into an assembler and keys in the mnemonic version of the program. The assembler uses whatever operator display which is available, e.g. CRT, VDU or segment display, to indicate any errors. An incorrect mnemonic may be rejected, or an incorrect syntax, e.g. comma in the wrong place, may be highlighted.

There are two types of assembler:

(1) Line-by-line assembler, which converts each instruction into

machine code as it is entered; comments (as shown above) cannot usually be entered.

(2) Full assembler, which waits until the entire program is entered and then creates an equivalent machine code version; normally comments can be entered and memorised with this type.

The second type is common with disk-based microcomputers. Both the "source code" (assembly language version) and the "object code" (machine code version) are stored on disk as separate files.

A more complicated program example, which uses a label, is as follows:

```
            MVI  A,1        ; Move (immediate) 1 into A
            OUT  10H        ; Output from A to input/output port
                              address hex. 10
            MVI  B,70       ; Move (immediate) delay loop count of
                              70 into B
REPEAT:     DCR  B          ; Decrement delay loop count (in B)
            JNZ  REPEAT     ; Jump if delay loop count (in B) is
                              not zero
            MVI  A,0        ; Move (immediate) 0 into A
            OUT  10H        ; Output from A to input/output port
                              address hex. 10
```

The program begins and ends by loading different bit patterns into the accumulator and outputting them to the same input/output address. The central three instructions demonstrate the classical method of generating a time delay by software—a register is loaded with a value, which is then decremented to zero in a two-instruction "loop" (notice the use of the label REPEAT). The action of the program is to set a 1 on a port output pin, delay for approximately 0.6 msec and then reset the signal to 0.

Good assemblers possess a powerful range of pseudo-instructions, or "pseudos", which greatly ease the programmer's task. A pseudo is a command to the assembler which does not cause the creation of a machine code instruction but instead instructs the assembler to perform some "housekeeping" role. Examples are:

ORG—(organiser) start assembling at a specific memory location

EQU—(equate) give a name or label to a memory address or data value
DB—(data byte) enter data values, not program instructions
END—(end) program is completed

A sample program which uses these features is:

```
         ORG 1000H        ; Start assembling at memory location
                            hex. 1000
TOM EQU 2000H             ; Set label TOM to hex. 2000
DICK EQU 2001H            ; Set label DICK to hex. 2001
BEGIN:IN    20H           ; Input from port address hex. 20 to A
      MOV B,A             ; Move A to B (temporary storage)
      LDA TOM             ; Load A with contents of TOM (2)
      CMP B               ; Compare A and B
      JZ   SKIP           ; Jump if same (literally "jump on zero")
      MOV A,B             ; Move B back to A (temporary storage)
      STA  DICK           ; Store A in DICK (memory address hex.
                            2001)
SKIP:JMP  BEGIN           ; Repeat program continuously
      ORG TOM             ; Transfer assembler control to TOM
                            (hex. 2000)
      DB   2              ; Insert data value 2 into TOM
      END                 ; Finish program listing
```

The program loops continuously. Firstly it reads in the setting of the 8 bits on input port address hex. 20 and compares this bit pattern with a data byte which is held in memory location hex. 2000 (called TOM). If the bit patterns are not the same (0000 0010), then the input reading is stored in memory location hex. 2001 (called DICK).

The program, which is loaded into memory commencing at location hex. 1000, begins with the IN instruction (labelled BEGIN) and ends with the JMP instruction (labelled SKIP). All other commands are pseudos.

Some even more powerful assemblers are called "macro assemblers" and offer an additional feature of allowing the programmer to specify a single name or label for a section of program. If the programmer then subsequently specifies that name in his program entry procedure, the assembler inserts the requisite program section.

7.2 HIGH-LEVEL LANGUAGES

A high-level language allows the programmer to write his program using statements which are similar to spoken language. Lengthy machine code programs can be expressed in short and readable high-level language form; this is unlike the 1:1 correspondence which exists between assembly language statements and machine code.

There are several high-level languages available for microcomputers, e.g. BASIC, PASCAL, FORTRAN, FORTH and many others, BASIC is by far the most popular. One big advantage of using high-level languages, apart from the speed and ease of programming, is that a program written for one machine can be readily transferred to another machine with only minor modifications. Clearly this does not apply to assembly language programs, which cannot be transferred from a machine which uses one type of microprocessor to another machine which uses a different type of CPU.

The drawbacks with high-level language programs are that they possess slow execution times and they cannot perform detailed input/output operations. This latter objection is overcome with many high-level languages by allowing the insertion of a machine code section within the high-level language program.

A program must already exist within a microcomputer, e.g. in ROM or on disk, to convert the high-level language program into machine code before it is run. There are two fundamentally different types of conversion program, as follows.

(a) Interpreter

This converts one statement at a time into machine code and executes the generated machine code at program run-time. It means that program execution times are extremely slow. However, since microcomputers are normally single-user machines, slow program implementation times are not a major drawback normally.

(b) Compiler

This converts the entire program into a machine code file, and stores that file on disk, prior to run-time. Hence two versions of the program exist. The machine code version is transferred from disk and run in memory when the program is called. Program operation is much faster than for a program which is run in an interpretive mode. However, compiled programs require more programmer operation prior to run-time in order to perform the separate compilation process.

Microcomputers often do not offer compilers. Most personal computers and home computers include only an interpreter, which is invariably BASIC. There are many versions of BASIC, but the same elementary commands are used in each.

A typical short BASIC program looks like:

```
10 REM PROGRAM TO CALCULATE SUM AND PRODUCT
20 X=100
30 Y=200
40 REM DISPLAY SUM
50 PRINT X+Y
60 REM DISPLAY PRODUCT
70 PRINT X*Y
80 END
```

Statements at lines 10, 40 and 60 are remark (REM) or comments statements. They are ignored when the program is run, but they make the program more readable. The names of the variables X and Y could be altered to TOM and DICK, for example, but they must begin with a letter. The PRINT command causes the value of a variable, or a text message, to appear on the CRT screen. Notice that statement numbers normally increment by 10, and this is to allow additional statements to be inserted later.

In some microcomputers which possess BASIC, the programmer can immediately enter such a program when the machine is switched on. In other machines the BASIC interpreter must first be called. After the program is entered it is executed by typing in RUN. Typical commands to store the program on disk, and to retrieve it later, are SAVE and LOAD.

The previous program can be made to be "interactive", i.e. it asks the operator to enter two numbers, as follows:

```
10 REM PROGRAM TO DISPLAY SUM AND PRODUCT OF
      ENTERED NUMBERS
```

```
20 PRINT "PLEASE ENTER TWO NUMBERS"
30 INPUT X,Y
40 REM NOW DISPLAY SUM
50 PRINT "SUM IS";X+Y
60 REM NOW DISPLAY PRODUCT
70 PRINT "PRODUCT IS";X*Y
80 END
```

When the program is run, it displays the message "PLEASE ENTER TWO NUMBERS" and then waits on line 30 until the operator keys in two numbers (separated by operation of the comma key and terminated by the RETURN key). It then proceeds to display the sum and product. The overall CRT screen on completion looks like:

```
PLEASE ENTER TWO NUMBERS
? 83,40
SUM IS     123
PRODUCT IS    3320
```

A more complicated program which uses a program loop (using the FOR and NEXT commands) and accesses a "data table" of numbers (using the DATA and READ commands) is as follows:

```
10 REM PROGRAM TO CALCULATE THE TOTAL AND
     MEAN OF 10 VALUES
20 TOTAL=0
30 FOR J=1 TO 10
40 READ FRED
50 TOTAL=TOTAL+FRED
60 NEXT
70 REM FINISHED PROCESSING NOW DISPLAY RESULTS
80 PRINT "TOTAL IS";TOTAL
90 PRINT "MEAN IS";TOTAL/10
100 DATA 16,4,85,2,39,46,1,9,72,54
110 END
```

When the program is run it loops between the FOR and NEXT commands for each value of J, i.e. 10 times. Within the loop, the READ command extracts each value from the DATA statement in turn and assigns the variable name FRED to that value. Therefore, when the program reaches line 70 the variable TOTAL holds the sum of all values in the DATA command. The PRINT commands display the answers of total and mean.

Several additional commands and facilities are available in BASIC. Examples are:

(i) IF—THEN, e.g.

```
180 IF TOM=25 THEN 260
```

This statement checks the value of the variable TOM. If it is 25 the program jumps to statement 260.

(ii) MATHEMATICAL FUNCTIONS, e.g.

```
930 SUSIE=SQR(ELSIE)
```

sets SUSIE to the square root of ELSIE.

(iii) DATA LISTS AND ARRAYS, e.g.

```
70 HARRY(I)=100
```

sets one of a list of data values called HARRY to 100, e.g. if I=3, then the third value is used.

```
560 TOM(3,5)=FRANK
```

sets one variable in an array of data values called TOM to the value of FRANK; the array TOM therefore has at least $3 \times 5 = 15$ values.

(iv) TEXT STRING, e.g.

```
690 WORDS$="THIS IS A TEST MESSAGE"
700 PRINT WORDS$
```

The string name must end with a $. The string can then be used, e.g. displayed several times later in the program, simply by referring to its name.

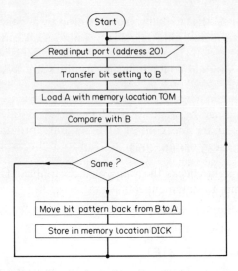

Fig. 7.1. Flow chart for last program in section 7.1.

7.3 FLOW CHARTS AND TRACE TABLES

A flow chart is a diagrammatic representation of program flow. It is often helpful to a programmer to design his program in flow chart form before he prepares the program listing in low- or high-level language. Experienced programmers often shun the use of this technique for most programming applications, but occasionally revert to the use of a flow chart for planning a particularly complex part of program logic.

Figure 7.1 shows a flow chart for the final program in section 7.1. Notice the standardised use of the following shapes:

    (a) Oval—for start and end of program (no end in this case because the program loops continuously).
    (b) Rectangle—for normal processing stages.
    (c) Rectangle with sloping sides—for input/output operation.
    (d) Diamond—this is a decision block, and has two exits.
    (e) Circle (not shown)—to indicate the continuation of a flow chart, e.g. if it is split into two or more pages.

Another useful programming aid is the use of a trace table. This means different things to different programmers. Basically it is a list of data values, e.g. in registers and/or memory locations, which occur at different stages in the execution of a program. Typically a programmer may make a list of data values which he expects at different points in his program under test, and then he checks these with actual values whilst he executes his program stage-by-stage in a "debugging" mode. This debugging procedure is under the control of a separate program which allows execution of the program under test up to a "breakpoint" or selected instruction, single-step (perform one instruction at a time), examine registers and memory locations, etc. This debugging program may be part of the monitor program or it may be a separate disk-based program in a large microcomputer system which possesses a floppy disk or hard disk.

7.4 SUBROUTINES AND INTERRUPTS

A subroutine is a section of program which is separated away from the main program and can be called more than once by the main program.

Figure 7.2 shows how a main program calls a subroutine twice. Entry to

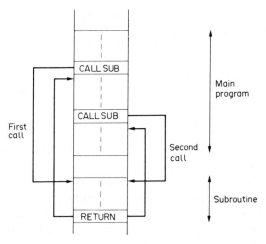

FIG. 7.2. Memory map of main program and subroutine.

the subroutine is by means of the

CALL SUB

assembly language instruction, where SUB is a label for the start address in memory of the subroutine.

The subroutine terminates with a

RET

instruction, which sends control back to the instruction in the main program which follows the CALL instruction. Therefore a mechanism must exist for storing return addresses. Since subroutine "nesting", i.e. one subroutine calls another, is possible with most microprocessors, this mechanism must allow for two or even more return addresses to be staticised. This is usually achieved by means of a "stack", as demonstrated in Fig. 7.3. A stack is an area of memory (RAM) which stores return addresses, and a CPU register, called the stack pointer, holds the address of the next free location in the stack. When the subroutine is called, the CPU automatically stores the return address on the stack (at the address held in the stack pointer) and decrements the stack pointer; invariably the stack expands backwards through memory. When the RET instruction at the end of the subroutine is executed, the return address is removed from the stack and placed in the CPU's program counter automatically, so that program execution can continue through the main program; the stack pointer is incremented to its original value.

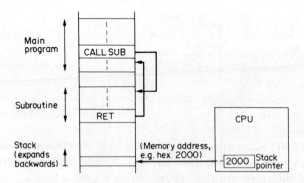

Fig. 7.3. Use of stack for subroutine call.

The principal advantage of the use of a subroutine is that a section of program, which is used on several occasions, needs only be entered once; thus it saves memory space. Also it makes programs more readable and easier to debug, because the overall program is fragmented into more manageable modules.

Sometimes program instructions can be used to store the contents of registers on the stack. Although this technique somewhat abuses the primary role of the stack (to store return addresses), it is easier to perform temporary storage of data items this way than to store them in specific memory locations (perhaps the programmer is unsure of where unused RAM exists for this data dumping). The instructions to use the stack in this manner are typically:

PUSH—to store a register/registers contents on the stack.
POP—to retrieve a register/registers contents off the stack.

The stack is also used to store return addresses when an interrupt routine is applied. An interrupt routine is a separate program which is held in memory to service the setting of an external hardware signal. CPUs possess several, typically four, interrupt lines which constitute part of the control bus. The role of an interrupt is to cause suspension of whatever program is running and to initiate immediate servicing. A unique address must be held by the CPU to indicate the start of each interrupt routine. This is performed normally using "interrupt vectors". Figure 7.4 shows how reserved memory locations contain the start addresses of the interrupt routines for a particular CPU. If an interrupt occurs at some unpredictable time during the operation of a main program, program control is transferred to the fixed memory location which contains the vector for that particular interrupt line. Also the return address is stored on the stack. The vector is a JUMP instruction which sends control into the interrupt routine. The final instruction in the interrupt routine is a RET instruction, which transfers control back to the main program. The main program then continues without being aware that it has been interrupted.

The CPU normally contains an interrupt mask, which can be set by software to block unwanted interrupts. Also it can be used to disrupt the normal interrupt priority system which requires that a lower priority interrupt cannot interrupt a higher priority interrupt.

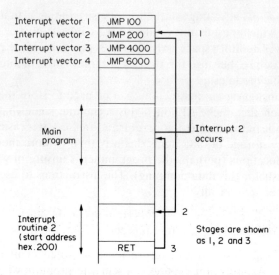

FIG. 7.4. Application of interrupt vector.

Interrupts are used commonly for the following applications:

(a) Power-up—when a delay circuit has allowed the DC rail voltages sufficient time to settle after machine switch-on, an interrupt is generated to cause entry into a specific point in the main program

(b) Timer—a regular pulse stream (probably from a counter/timer on a PIO) can generate an interrupt, so that the servicing interrupt routine can update a time count, e.g. to update a time-of-day clock in memory

(c) Floppy disk—when a disk has completed data transfer an interrupt signal can be generated

(d) Keyboard—a keyboard encoder (see section 6.2) can generate an interrupt pulse which causes entry into an interrupt routine only when a key is pressed.

7.5 ADDRESSING MODES

Microprocessors offer a variety of methods of accessing data items within instructions. These methods are called "addressing modes", and normally a large number of addressing modes assists the programmer and increases the "power" of the microprocessor.

When a data item is transferred from one register or memory location to another (perhaps with processing in the CPU's Arithmetic and Logic Unit, e.g. add, shift, AND), then different addressing modes can be selected for both the source and destination. The principal addressing modes are as follow (using Intel 8080/8085 mnemonics).

(a) Direct Addressing

This is the simplest mode, and it involves data transfer directly between register and register or between register and memory location, e.g.

MOV C,A

moves the contents of register A (accumulator) to register C. In this case both source and destination addressing modes are "direct register".

The other type of direct addressing is:

LDA 1600H

which moves the contents of memory location hex. 1600 into the A register (accumulator). In this case the source (memory location hex. 1600) is referenced by "direct memory" addressing. The destination (A register) uses direct register addressing.

(b) Indirect Addressing

In the indirect addressing mode, the source or destination is not a straightforward register or memory location. Instead the specified register or memory location *contains* the memory address of the data item. Therefore the register or memory location "points to" the memory address of the value. For example:

MOV B,M

moves into the B register the data value whose memory location is held in the HL register-pair (referred to in the instruction by the letter M). Therefore the source (M) is "indirect register" addressing. The destination (B register) uses direct register addressing.

Indirect memory addressing is not found commonly with microprocessors. However, the reader can visualise its operation.

(c) Immediate Addressing

In this mode the data item is not contained within a register or a memory location, but is held in the instruction itself, e.g.

MVI B,6

moves the data value 6 into the B register. Clearly this instruction is double-word, with the data value 6 filling the second word or byte.

(d) Indexed Addressing

This addressing mode is not found in all 8-bit microprocessors (e.g. the Intel 8080/8085), but it is extremely powerful, e.g.

MOV R2,1000H(R4)   (not on Intel 8080/8085)

moves the contents of memory location hex. 1000 (direct memory) *plus* the contents of register 4, to register 2. Therefore the source address is an amalgam of a memory location and the contents of a register, and an addition process must be carried out within the instruction before data transfer can occur.

Whilst these are the primary addressing modes which are performed when data values are transferred or processed, different types of addressing modes are used with jump instructions, as follows.

(e) Absolute Addressing

For example,

JZ 4400H

jumps on zero to the instruction at memory location hex. 4400. This mode is normally used also with subroutine calls, e.g. CALL 2000H.

(f) Relative Addressing

JNZ +15   (not on Intel 8080/8085)

jumps on non-zero to the instruction which is 15 words further on. The value of this particular addressing mode is that the programmer can forget about absolute memory addresses. Also the program can be relocated anywhere in memory since specific memory addresses are not used.

The reader should note that further addressing modes are applied within different microprocessors, e.g. "paged" addressing, "segment" addressing. Reference should be made to the manufacturer's information sheets for the specific CPU if these modes are utilised.

7.6 MEMORY MAPPED INPUT/OUTPUT

Sometimes input/output chips are connected into a microcomputer circuit in the same manner as memory ICs. They are then accessed using memory transfer instructions instead of input/output instructions (e.g. IN and OUT). This is termed "memory mapped" input/output.

Consider the circuit arrangement of Fig. 7.5. Outputs from a shared address decoder circuit feed chip select signals for both input/output and

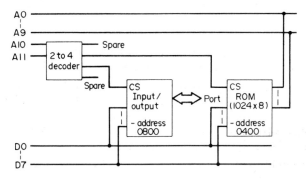

Fig. 7.5. Memory mapped input/output circuit arrangement.

memory chips. (The reader may like to check his understanding of address decoding by confirming the addresses hex. 0400 and 0800.) The advantage of this arrangement is for ease of programming. The same instructions are used for both input/output and memory transfers, and a larger and more flexible set of instructions is available for input and output operations, e.g.

LDA 0800H
MOV A,M   (if HL contains 0800)   } if port is input

STA 0800H
MOV M,A   (if HL contains 0800)   } if port is output

A hardware gain is that fewer address decoder chips are required.

The disadvantage is that input/output uses up memory addresses, e.g. hex. 0800 to 0C00 in the example above—hex. 400 addresses for a single port.

Memory mapped input/output is commonly applied with personal computers, e.g. the Commodore PET, Apple and BBC computer. This means that the programmer can apply the same BASIC commands to examine (PEEK) and alter (POKE) memory locations and to implement input and output operations, e.g.

READING=PEEK(1024)—if port is input in example above (input from port and call bit pattern the variable name READING).

POKE 1024,1—if port is output in example above (outputs a bit pattern 0000 0001 to the port).

Notice that address hex. 0800 is expressed in decimal (1024).

7.7 PROGRAM DEVELOPMENT

If a new high-level language program is required for a personal computer, e.g. a commercial or business program, then it can normally be entered and developed on the same machine. If a new low-level language program is required for a single-board application, e.g. washing machine controller or telephone answering machine, then program development is normally performed on a separate microprocessor development system

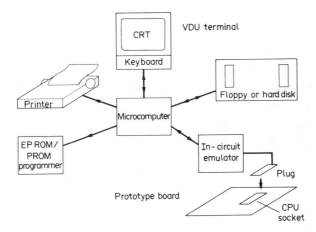

FIG. 7.6. Microprocessor development system (MDS).

(MDS). When the new program is fully tested it is then transferred on EPROM or PROM to the prototype board.

The hardware features of an MDS are shown in Fig. 7.6. The system clearly is based on the same CPU as used in the prototype board. A terminal (VDU) provides the operator interface, and floppy or hard disk is used for program and file storage. A printer is required to produce a listing of the developed program, and an EPROM/PROM programmer is applied to enable the developed program to be transferred into the prototype board. The in-circuit emulator is a specialised device which allows the programmer to run the developed program in the MDS but to use the hardware of the prototype board; the connection between in-circuit emulator and prototype board is by means of a plug (40-pin typically) which fits into the CPU socket of the prototype board.

The software facilities within the MDS are as follow.

(a) Operating System

This is the main controller program which runs all others. It implements commands which the operator enters via the keyboard, and controls input/output operations to/from disk, printer, etc.

When the machine is switched on this program is loaded down from disk under control of a "bootstrap loader" program, which is normally ROM-based.

A large number of operating systems have been developed by different manufacturers. The Intel Intellec MDSs use the ISIS operating system. An extremely popular operating system, which is used in many personal computers as well as MDSs, is CP/M. This is applied principally with Intel 8080, 8085 and Zilog Z80 systems.

Facilities within the operating system allow the operator to display the names of all programs (often called "files") within the system, erase any file, print any file, make a second disk copy of a file, run any program, etc.

(b) Editor

The editor is a separate program which the user can call via the operating system, and it allows him to enter and alter a program or file.

(c) Assembler

The assembler converts an assembly language source file into a machine code file. If errors exist in the source program, the process is aborted and the errors are reported to the operator on the VDU.

(d) Loader

This loads the assembled machine code file into memory from disk.

(e) Debugger

The debugging or "trace" program allows the operator to run part or all of the program under test in a controlled manner in order to locate software faults. These facilities include execute, execute to a breakpoint, single step (obey one instruction only), examine/display registers and memory locations, etc.

(f) Linker

A facility often exists to "link" separate program sections, perhaps from a library of routines, in the user's program.

(g) EPROM/PROM Programmer

This program copies the fully tested program byte-by-byte into EPROM/PROM.

(h) In-circuit Emulator

An in-circuit emulator control program includes the same types of facilities as a debugger—see (e) above. Therefore the prototype program can be manipulated and executed within the MDS, whilst the memory and input/output circuitry of the prototype hardware board can be included in the testing procedure.

BIBLIOGRAPHY

1. *Microprocessors and Programmed Logic*. Kenneth L. Short. Prentice-Hall, 1981.
2. *Microprocessor Software*. G. A. Streitmatter. Prentice-Hall, 1981.
3. *BASIC Programming Primer*. Mitchell Waite and Michael Pardee. Prentice-Hall, 1978.
4. *From Chips to Systems*. Rodnay Zaks. Sybex, 1981.
5. *Study Notes for Technicians: Microprocessor Based Systems, Levels 4 and 5*. R. C. Holland. McGraw-Hill, 1984.

CHAPTER 8

Interfacing the
Intel 8085 Microprocessor

8.1 THE 8085 MICROPROCESSOR

The Intel 8085A (hereafter called simply the 8085) is one of the most popular 8-bit microprocessors. It is a descendant of the 8080, and was the model for the design of the Zilog Z80, which possesses several additional features to the 8085. Programs which run on the 8085 also run on the Z80.

The device requires only a single power supply ($+5$ V) and possesses an on-chip clock circuit, i.e. only a crystal is connected to the device to generate the CPU clock.

The internal organisation of the device is shown in Fig. 8.1. The program counter and the stack pointer are 16 bits and all other modules are 8 bits. The usual modules of instruction register, control unit and ALU are present, and the device uses seven registers. One particular register—the A register—receives the result of most of the complicated ALU operations, and hence is called the accumulator.

The 8085 possesses a characteristic which is unusual with 8-bit microprocessors but occurs frequently with 16-bit microprocessors, e.g. the Intel 8086 and the Zilog Z8001. The data bus and one-half of the address bus are multiplexed, i.e. they share the same pins in the 40-pin package. As we will see later in this chapter, several of its support input/output chips accept the two buses in this multiplexed form. However, if standard memory devices are connected, then the buses must be de-multiplexed using external circuitry.

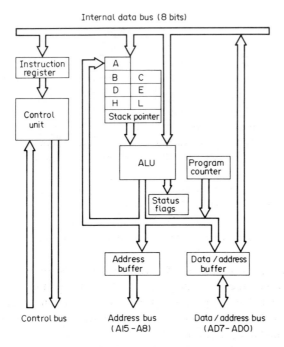

FIG. 8.1. The Intel 8085 microprocessor.

Instruction execution times vary from 1.3 μsec to 5.75 μsec for a 3.125 MHz clock (6.25 MHz input frequency). The device possesses five status bits: Zero (Z), Sign (S), Parity (P), Carry (C) and Auxiliary Carry (AC).

There are five interrupts: TRAP, RST 5.5, RST 6.5, RST 7.5 and INTR. TRAP is the highest priority interrupt signal and is non-maskable.

An extremely unusual feature of the 8085 is that it possesses a primitive form of serial input and output. A single-bit output and a single-bit input signal line (SOD and SID) can be used under software control to generate serial bit streams. However, these signals are more useful as single-signal output and input lines.

The pin connections are shown in Fig. 8.2. A brief description of the functions of the signals is given in the diagram. Notice that an unusually

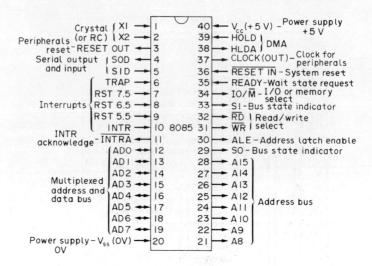

FIG. 8.2. 8085 pin connections.

large number of control bus lines are available because the data and one-half of the address buses are multiplexed. The ALE (address latch enable) signal is used to identify whether these eight multiplexed lines carry address or data signals (set high for address).

Table 8.1 lists the instruction set for the 8085. Notice from the first two groups (Move and Modify) that several instructions allow register-pair operation. For example, the instruction:

LXI B,0F3BH   (H means hexadecimal)

loads the register-pair B and C with the 16-bit number hex. 0F3B (0F enters B and 3B enters C), whilst:

DCX B

decrements the register-pair B and C to 0F3A.

Thus some 16-bit data manipulation is available in this 8-bit CPU.

Like most 8-bit microprocessors the 8085 offers only a limited number of addressing modes, i.e. methods of accessing data items, as shown on p. 119.

115

TABLE 8.1 INTEL 8085 INSTRUCTION SET

Mnemonic	Description
(a) *Move*	
MOVE, LOAD and STORE	
MOV r1,r2	Move register 2 to register 1
MOV M,r	Move register to memory
MOV r,M	Move memory to register
MVI r	Move immediate
MVI M	Move immediate memory
LXI B	Load immediate register-pair B & C
LXI D	Load immediate register-pair D & E
LXI H	Load immediate register-pair H & L
LXI SP	Load immediate stack pointer
STAX B	Store A indirect (using B & C)
STAX D	Store A indirect (using D & E)
LDAX B	Load A indirect (using B & C)
LDAX D	Load A indirect (using D & E)
STA	Store A direct
LDA	Load A direct
SHLD	Store H & L direct
LHLD	Load H & L direct
XCHG	Exchange D & E and H & L registers
INPUT/OUTPUT	
IN	Input
OUT	Output
(b) *Modify*	
INCREMENT and DECREMENT	
INR r	Increment register
DCR r	Decrement register
INR M	Increment memory
DCR M	Decrement memory
INX B	Increment B & C registers
INX D	Increment D & E registers
INX H	Increment H & L registers
INX SP	Increment stack pointer
DCX B	Decrement B & C
DCX D	Decrement D & E
DCX H	Decrement H & L
DCX SP	Decrement stack pointer
ADD	
ADD r	Add register to A
ADC r	Add register to A with carry

continued overleaf

TABLE 8.1 (contd.)

Mnemonic	Description
ADD M	Add memory to A
ADC M	Add memory to A with carry
ADI	Add immediate to A
ACI	Add immediate to A with carry
DAD B	Add B & C to H & L
DAD D	Add D & E to H & L
DAD H	Add H & L to H & L
DAD SP	Add stack pointer to H & L
SUBTRACT	
SUB r	Subtract register from A
SBB r	Subtract register from A with borrow
SUB M	Subtract memory from A
SBB M	Subtract memory from A with borrow
SUI	Subtract immediate from A
SBI	Subtract immediate from A with borrow
LOGICAL	
ANA r	AND register with A
XRA r	EXCLUSIVE OR register with A
ORA r	OR register with A
CMP r	Compare register with A
ANA M	AND memory with A
XRA M	EXCLUSIVE OR memory with A
ORA M	OR memory with A
CMP M	Compare memory with A
ANI	AND immediate with A
XRI	EXCLUSIVE OR immediate with A
ORI	OR immediate with A
CPI	Compare immediate with A
ROTATE	
RLC	Rotate A left
RRC	Rotate A right
RAL	Rotate A left through carry
RAR	Rotate A right through carry
SPECIALS	
CMA	Complement A
STC	Set carry
CMC	Complement carry
DAA	Decimal adjust A

Mnemonic	Description
(c) *Jump*	
JUMP	
JMP	Jump unconditional
JC	Jump on carry
JNC	Jump on no carry
JZ	Jump on zero
JNZ	Jump on no zero
JP	Jump on positive
JM	Jump on minus
JPE	Jump on parity even
JPO	Jump on parity odd
PCHL	H & L to program counter
(d) *Subroutine*	
CALL	
CALL	Call unconditional
CC	Call on carry
CNC	Call on no carry
CZ	Call on zero
CNZ	Call on no zero
CP	Call on positive
CM	Call on minus
CPE	Call on parity even
CPO	Call on parity odd
RETURN	
RET	Return
RC	Return on carry
RNC	Return on no carry
RZ	Return on zero
RNZ	Return on no zero
RP	Return on positive
RM	Return on minus
RPE	Return on parity even
RPO	Return on parity odd
(e) *Stack*	
STACK	
PUSH B	Push register-pair B & C on stack
PUSH D	Push register-pair D & E on stack
PUSH H	Push register-pair H & L on stack
PUSH PSW	Push A and flags on stack

continued overleaf

TABLE 8.1 (contd.)

Mnemonic	Description
POP B	Pop register-pair B & C off stack
POP D	Pop register-pair D & E off stack
POP H	Pop register-pair H & L off stack
POP PSW	Pop A and flags off stack
XTHL	Exchange top of stack and H & L
SPHL	H & L to stack pointer

(f) *Interrupts and Control*
INTERRUPTS

EI	Enable interrupts
DI	Disable interrupts
RIM	Read interrupt mask
SIM	Set interrupt mask

CONTROL

NOP	No-operation
HLT	Halt
RST	Restart

DDD or SSS

B–000
C–001
D–010
E–011
H–100
L–101
Memory–110
A–111

(a) Register Direct Addressing

e.g.   MOV C,A

moves the contents of A into C

or   INR A

increments (adds 1) A.

(b) Register Indirect Addressing

e.g.   LDAX B

loads into A from the memory address which is held in the BC register-pair

or   MOV A,M

moves into A from the memory address which is held in the HL register-pair (M = HL register-pair).

(c) Memory Direct Addressing

e.g.   LDA 5000H

loads into A from the memory address hex. 5000 (this is a 3-byte instruction; 5000 is stored in the second and third bytes).

(d) Immediate Addressing

e.g.   MVI A,4

moves the number 4 into A (this is a 2-byte instruction; 4 is stored in the second byte).

(e) Absolute Memory Addressing (for transferring program control)

This mode is used with JUMP and CALL instructions.

e.g.   JMP 0A30H

jumps unconditionally to the program instruction at memory location
hex. 0A30.

Consider the following sample program, which adds 8 numbers which
are loaded into memory starting at hex. 8000:

LXI H,8000H	;Load HL with memory address 8000
MVI A,0	;Clear A
MVI D,8	;Set loop count in D
REPEAT:ADD M	;Add from memory (contents of HL) into A
INX H	;Increment HL (point to next number)
DCR D	;Decrement loop count
JNZ REPEAT	;Repeat (total of 8 times)
MOV B,A	;Move answer from A to B
HERE:JMP HERE	;Loop stop on this instruction

The program uses three immediate addressing mode instructions to set up
registers. It then enters a program loop; each pass of the loop adds one of
the data values into a running total in A register. At the end of the loop
the answer is transferred to B. The last instruction "loop stops", or jumps
to itself, so that program control cannot proceed (an alternative instruction which performs the same function is HLT).

8.2 THE INTEL 8155 PIO

The 8155 is offered by Intel as a combined PIO and RAM device—the
256 bytes of RAM are an unusual bonus compared with PIOs from other
manufacturers.

Figure 8.3 shows the functions which are available on the 8155, and its
interconnection with a 8085 CPU. There are three programmable ports,
a counter/timer and 256 bytes of RAM on the 8155. The multiplexed data
and address buses are connected directly from the 8085.

The $\overline{RD}$ and $\overline{WR}$ (note inverse logic indicated by bar above symbols)
signals are used by the CPU to select direction of data transfer. The
IO/$\overline{M}$ selects input/output or memory. The RESET signal sets all ports to
input and clears the counter/timer to zero. The TIMER IN carries the

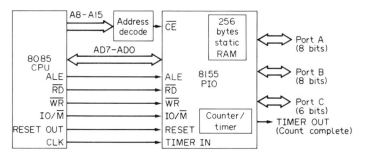

FIG. 8.3. The Intel 8155 PIO.

CPU clock to the counter/timer. The ALE signal identifies address or data on the multiplexed AD0–AD7 lines.

There are six input/output addresses on the device as follows:

AD2	AD1	AD0	
0	0	0	Control register
0	0	1	Port A
0	1	0	Port B
0	1	1	Port C
1	0	0	Counter/timer (low-order byte)
1	0	1	Counter/timer (high-order byte)

Control bytes are sent to the control register to initialise the ports as input or output, and also to select the mode of operation of the counter/timer. The control register is detailed in Fig. 8.4.

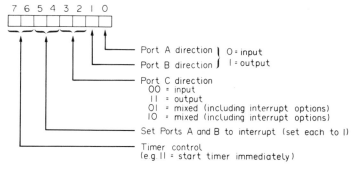

FIG. 8.4. Control register for 8155.

Therefore, if

0000 1110

is output to the control register, then Port A is selected as input and Ports B and C are selected as output.

When an input or output instruction is executed, the 8085 sends out the eight least significant address bits to AD7 to AD0 (e.g. to select one of the six addresses above) and also to A15 to A8 for address decoding. Therefore, if the address decoding circuit of Fig. 8.5 is used, the first of the input/output addresses (i.e. control register) is:

A15	A14	A13	A12	A11	A10	A9	A8		A7	A6	A5	A4	A3	A2	A1	A0
1	0	X	X	X	0	0	0		1	0	X	X	X	0	0	0

Address decoder   Input/output address hex. 80

(X = not used—say 0)

The control register address is hex. 80 therefore, Port A is 81, and so on.

Therefore the following program sets Ports A and B as output and Port C as input, and then outputs all 1s to Port B:

MVI A,03H
OUT 80H
MVI A,FFH
OUT 82H

The counter/timer can be set to generate a precise delay of 1 msec by sending it a 14-bit count as follows:

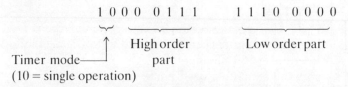

1 0 0 0   0 1 1 1   1 1 1 0   0 0 0 0

High order part   Low order part

Timer mode
(10 = single operation)

The count of hex. 07E0 equates to decimal 2000, and if the CPU clock (TIMER IN) pulse speed is 2 MHz (0.5 μsec interval) the total delay is:

$$2000 \times 0.5 \times 10^{-6} = 10^{-3} = 1 \text{ msec.}$$

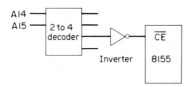

FIG. 8.5. Typical address decoder for 8155.

Therefore the following program activates the timer:

```
MVI  A,E0H      ;Output E0 to
OUT  84H        ;               low order part of counter/timer
MVI  A,87H      ;Output 87 to
OUT  85H        ;               high order part of counter/timer
MVI  A,C0H      ;Output C0 to
OUT  80H        ;               control register
```

The timer Count Complete (TIMER OUT) signal can then be scanned (or "polled") in order to generate the 1 msec delay, or it can be connected to an interrupt line so that an interrupt program is called after 1 msec. If the Count Complete is connected to the RST 6.5 interrupt line, which requires its interrupt vector at memory location hex. 0034, then a jump instruction (jump to start address of interrupt program) must be inserted at location 0034. If the 2-bit timer mode setting is 11 in place of 10 then the counter/timer repeatedly resets itself and counts down again. Thus an interrupt is generated every 1 msec continuously.

8.3 THE INTEL 8251A USART

The 8251A USART (universal synchronous/asynchronous receiver/transmitter) is a serial interfacing device which is used by Intel and other manufacturers to interface microcomputers to VDUs, printers and other computers. The synchronous mode is rarely used.

The interconnection signals are shown in Fig. 8.6. The function of $\overline{RD}$, $\overline{WR}$ and RESET are the same as for the 8155; after a RESET the USART must be re-initialised. The CLK input must carry pulses which operate at a frequency greater than 30 times the transmit or receive baud rates, and

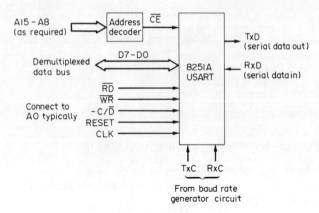

FIG. 8.6. The Intel 8251A USART.

is derived from the CPU clock normally. The TxC and RxC signals are the transmit and receive clocks which determine the baud rate of data transfer.

Effectively there are four addresses on the chip and one may expect to see two address lines A0 and A1 connected—this does not occur. These apparent addresses are:

| Selected when $C/\overline{D}$ (A0) is 0 | $\begin{cases}$ Transmit data—selected by $\overline{WR}$ (at 0) \\ Receive data—selected by $\overline{R D}$ (at 0)$\end{cases}$ |
| Selected when $C/\overline{D}$ (A0) is 1 | $\begin{cases}$ Control register—selected by $\overline{W R}$ (at 0) \\ Status register—selected by $\overline{R D}$ (at 0)$\end{cases}$ |

Therefore the $C/\overline{D}$ (control/data) signal selects the device in its data transmit/receive mode or in its control mode (i.e. to initialise the device for baud rate, etc.). Sensibly $C/\overline{D}$ is connected to the least-significant address line A0. The direction of the data transfer is determined by the settings of the $\overline{R D}$ and $\overline{W R}$ signals, e.g. a 1 and a 0 respectively are set by the OUT instruction, and the converse levels are set by the IN instruction. Thus the connection on only one address line (A0 to $C/\overline{D}$) suffices to provide selection of one of the four addresses.

The methods of connection to a VDU, and a remote VDU or another computer using a modem, are shown in Fig. 8.7. In (a) the standard RS

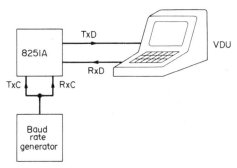

(a) Connection to VDU terminal

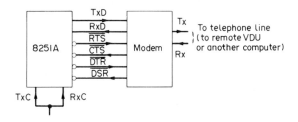

(b) Connection to remote device via a modem

Fig. 8.7. Connection of 8251A to serial peripherals.

232-C connections are made for Tx and Rx (and 0 V) at the VDU. The 8251A is fed with the same baud rate clock signals on TxC and RxC since transmit and receive baud rates are the same.

In (b) the modem modulates a sinewave carrier (e.g. 1 = 1180 Hz, 0 = 980 Hz) so that bits are transmitted as different frequencies over the telephone link. Additionally "handshaking" is introduced between the 8251A and the modem. The 8251A generates a $\overline{RTS}$ signal (request to send) and the modem replies with $\overline{CTS}$ (clear to send) before a character is transmitted. Also the modem can be asked if it is receiving a carrier frequency (which effectively includes a check on whether the remote device is switched on) by the 8251A generating a $\overline{DSR}$ (data set ready) and the modem replying with a $\overline{DTR}$ (data terminal ready).

Although synchronous transfer is rare, it is worth indicating the minor

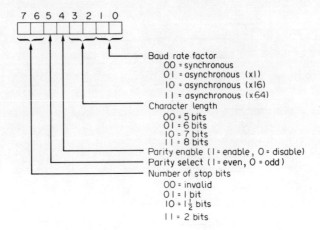

Fig. 8.8. Control register for 8251A USART.

change which is necessary to the above arrangements which are used for asynchronous transfer. The RxC and TxC signals are linked together and connect to the same signals at the other end of the link, i.e. the 8251A and the remote peripheral (or other computer) share the same clock. Start and stop bits are not generated in this mode of operation.

The method of initialising an 8251A to select baud rate, number of stop bits, etc., is by sending a control byte to the control register, which is described in Fig. 8.8. Thus if the device has an address of hex. 04, the following program:

```
MVI  A,7AH      ;Bit pattern 0111 1010
OUT  04H        ;Output to control register (initialise)
```

sets the number of stop bits to 1, parity to even and the character length to 7 bits. The baud rate factor is set to x16, i.e. if the incoming TxC and RxC signals are at 38.4 kHz then the transmit and receive baud rates are:

$$\frac{38400}{16} = 2400 \text{ baud.}$$

Although the 8251A appears to be offering three different programmable baud rate settings ($\times 1$, $\times 16$, $\times 64$), the magnitude of the jump from one setting to the next effectively means that at best only two baud rates are realisable. If the full range of standard baud rates is required, e.g. 300, 600, 1200, 2400, 4800, etc., then a mechanism must exist for switching the frequencies of the baud rate generator. This can be achieved by means of links or jumpers associated with the multivibrator circuit, or by using a programmable generator, e.g. the 8224, which can be set to different frequencies by software.

The status register can be used by software to check the status of the 8251A, e.g. parity error, Tx ready (last transmit character cleared), overrun error (previous character not read by CPU before next one is received), etc.

The following example program outputs two ASCII characters for M and N to a VDU which is driven by an 8251A at input/output address hex. 60. Firstly the USART is initialised to run at 1200 baud (baud rate generator runs at 76.8 kHz), with disabled parity, 7 data bits and $1\frac{1}{2}$ stop bits.

```
        MVI  A,8BH      ;Bit pattern 1000 1011
        OUT  61H        ;Output to control register (initialise)
        MVI  A,4DH      ;ASCII for M
        OUT  60H        ;Send M to VDU
POLL:IN      61H        ;Poll status register
        ANI  1          ;Mask out all bits except Tx ready
        JZ   POLL       ;Continually poll until M is cleared
        MVI  A,4EH      ;ASCII for N
        OUT  60H        ;Send N to VDU
```

8.4 EXAMPLES

Intel supply a range of input/output chips in addition to the flexible 8155 and 8251A, which have just been described. The following is a selection:

(1) 8212—non-programmable input/output port
(2) 8253—triple counter/timer
(3) 8255—programmable three ports
(4) 8355—programmable two ports plus 2048 bytes of ROM
and several others.

We will finish this survey of the Intel 8085 and its interfacing circuitry with some programming examples.

(a) Lighting a LED

If a LED is driven by the least significant bit (top output) of a port address hex. 40, then the following program section sets its drive signal to 1:

```
MVI   A,1      ;Bit pattern 0000 0001
OUT  40H       ;Port address
```

(b) Driving a Stepper Motor

If a stepper motor is connected to a port as shown in Fig. 8.9, then the following program rotates the motor by one revolution in a clockwise direction:

```
          MVI   B,48      ;Loop count (48 pulses per
                                revolution)
    LOOP:MVI   A,3        ;Bit pattern 0000 0011
          OUT   10H       ;Output a 1 for leading edge of pulse
          CALL  DELAY     ;Delay (1 millisecond)
          MVI   A,2        ;Bit pattern 0000 0010
          OUT   10H       ;Output a 0 for trailing edge of pulse
          CALL  DELAY     ;Delay (1 millisecond)
          DCR   B          ;Decrement loop count (number of
                                pulses)
          JNZ   LOOP       ;Repeat (total of 48 pulses)
          HLT               ;Stop on this instruction
  DELAY:MVI   C,142      ;Delay loop count
 REPEAT:DCR   C           ;Count down
          JNZ   REPEAT     ;          delay count
                                (total = 1 millisecond)
          RET               ;Return to main program
```

The reader may like to suggest minor changes to this program to cause the

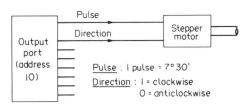

FIG. 8.9. Connection to a stepper motor.

stepper motor to rotate half a revolution in an anti-clockwise direction. Also more significant changes may be examined to cause the motor to rotate continuously. How is the speed of rotation varied?

(c) Driving a Segment Display and Scanning a Keyboard

Examine the circuit arrangement of Fig. 4.12 and assume that it is connected to an Intel 8155 with port addresses of hex. 20, 21 and 22. The following program displays the character 2 (i.e. segments a, b, g, e and d) on the right-hand display digit:

```
MVI   A,5BH      ;Segment pattern 0101 1011
OUT   20H        ;Output to segments
MVI   A,13       ;Digit line setting 0001 0011
OUT   21H        ;Output to set last digit line
```

A program which polls the left-hand column of keys until it detects that a key is pressed is:

```
      MVI   A,0      ;Digit line setting of 0000 0000
      OUT   21H      ;Output to set first digit line
POLL:IN    22H      ;Input settings of left-hand column of keys
      JZ    POLL     ;Repeat until a key is pressed
```

BIBLIOGRAPHY

1. *An Introduction to Microcomputers*, Vol. 2. A. Osborne. Osborne, 1978.
2. *8085A Cookbook*. Jonathan A. Titus, Christopher A. Titus and David G. Larsen. Prentice-Hall, 1980.
3. *Microprocessors and Microcomputers*. B. G. Woollard. McGraw-Hill, 1982.

CHAPTER 9

Interfacing the
Zilog Z80 Microprocessor

9.1 THE Z80 MICROPROCESSOR

The Zilog Z80 is arguably the most powerful 8-bit microprocessor. It was designed by a breakaway team of engineers from Intel and was intended to be an update on the Intel 8080. In fact it has improved features over the later Intel 8085A. Its instruction set includes all of the instructions which the 8080 and 8085 possess, plus several more. Programs written in machine code for the Intel devices will run on the Z80 without modification. Compatibility in the reverse direction cannot be guaranteed because the Z80 possesses additional instructions.

Figure 9.1 shows the internal organisation of the Z80. Registers A, B, C, D, E, H and L and the status flags are as used in the 8085. Additionally the Z80 possesses a duplicate set of these registers (A', B', etc.). This gives the considerable advantage with the Zilog device that the second set can be selected within an interrupt routine; this avoids the necessity of storing off the contents of work registers (probably on the stack) when the interrupt routine is entered.

Another advantage of the Z80 over the 8085 is that the address and data buses are not multiplexed, i.e. they do not share the same pins on the 40-pin package.

The Z80 possesses four additional registers to the 8085—the refresh register, two index registers and the interrupt register. The memory refresh register is an unusual bonus feature with a microprocessor and it is used to refresh any dynamic RAM which may be included in the

Internal data bus (8 bits)

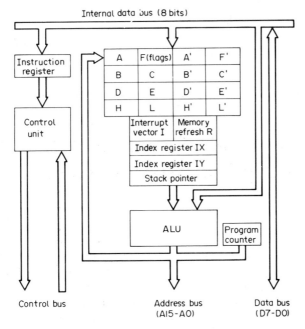

FIG. 9.1. The Zilog Z80 microprocessor.

microcomputer system. Simply it is a 7-bit counter which is incremented automatically during each fetch/execute cycle. Simultaneously this count is presented on the address bus together with a special control bus signal (RFSH) so that dynamic RAM devices can be refreshed.

The index registers allow indexed addressing, which is not available with the 8085. The other additional addressing mode which is offered is program relative jump instructions, and these two additional addressing modes are described as follows.

(a) Indexed Addressing

Indexed addressing adds a single-byte displacement, which is included in the instruction, to the contents of one of the indexing registers IX or IY,

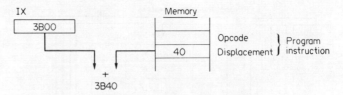

FIG. 9.2. Example of Z80 indexed addressing (using IX register).

as shown in Fig. 9.2. For the example shown it is assumed that a previous instruction in the program loaded hex. 3B00 into the IX index register. The indexed addressing instruction uses this base address and modifies it by the displacement byte hex. 40, which is contained in the instruction. The memory location 3B40 is then accessed in the instruction.

(b) Program Relative Jump Instruction

In this addressing mode, a single-byte displacement is provided by the instruction and this is added to the program counter if the jump is successful.

The pin layout of the Z80 is shown in Fig. 9.3. A single power supply (+5 V and 0 V) is required, and the usual DMA and read/write control signals are available. The device requires a separate clock circuit.

At first sight the Z80 appears to possess a more limited interrupt capability than the 8085 since only two interrupt signals ($\overline{INT}$—interrupt request, and $\overline{NMI}$—non-maskable interrupt request) are used in place of the five 8085 signals. However the following options are available for handling interrupts.

(1) $\overline{RESET}$. The reset signal is used conveniently as a power-up interrupt since apart from resetting the interrupt vector and refresh register, the program counter is forced to 0000.
(2) $\overline{NMI}$. When this signal goes low, an interrupt routine at a fixed address of hex. 0066 is entered.

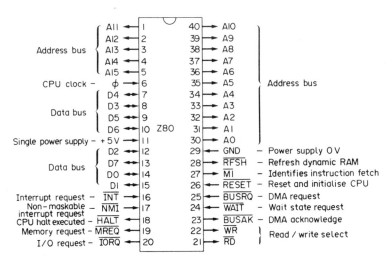

FIG. 9.3. Z80 pin connections.

(3) $\overline{\text{INT}}$. This interrupt line is a lower priority than $\overline{\text{NMI}}$. Its setting causes different responses by the CPU, depending on which of the three interrupt modes has been selected for the CPU—a single program instruction at the start of a main program normally selects one of these modes. In mode 0 the contents of the interrupt vector are interpreted as a single-byte object code. In mode 1 an interrupt routine at a fixed memory location of hex. 0056 is entered. In mode 2 the interrupting device must generate one-half of the interrupt vector which points to the interrupt routine; the other (most significant) half, or byte, is supplied by the contents of the interrupt vector register within the CPU. For example, if the interrupt vector register has been set by a program instruction to hold hex. 20 and the interrupting device (e.g. a PIO) places hex. 60 on the data bus, then the CPU examines location hex. 2060 to find the start address of the interrupt routine.

The instruction set for the Z80 is listed in Table 9.1. There is no doubt that many novice programmers are intimidated by the complexity of this instruction set and the range of powerful features which it offers.

TABLE 9.1 ZILOG Z80 INSTRUCTION SET

Mnemonics	Description
ADC HL,ss	Add with Carry Reg. pair ss to HL
ADC A,s	Add with carry operand s to Acc.
ADD A,n	Add value n to Acc.
ADD A,r	Add Reg. r to Acc.
ADD A,(HL)	Add location (HL) to Acc.
ADD A,(IX+d)	Add location (IX+d) to Acc.
ADD A,(IY+d)	Add location (IY+d) to Acc.
ADD HL,ss	Add Reg. pair ss to HL
ADD IX,pp	Add Reg. pair pp to IX
ADD IY,rr	Add Reg. pair rr to IY
AND s	Logical "AND" of operand s and Acc.
BIT b,(HL)	Test BIT b of location (HL)
BIT b,(IX+d)	Test BIT b of location (IX+d)
BIT b,(IY+d)	Test BIT b of location (IY+d)
BIT b,r	Test BIT b of Reg. r
CALL cc,nn	Call subroutine at location nn if condition cc is true
CALL nn	Unconditional call subroutine at location nn
CCF	Complement carry flag
CP s	Compare operand s with Acc.
CPD	Compare location (HL) and Acc. decrement HL and BC
CPDR	Compare location (HL) and Acc. decrement HL and BC, repeat until BC=0
CPI	Compare location (HL) and Acc. increment HL and decrement BC
CPIR	Compare location (HL) and Acc. increment HL, decrement BC repeat until BC=0
CPL	Complement Acc. (1s comp)
DAA	Decimal adjust Acc.
DEC m	Decrement operand m
DEC IX	Decrement IX
DEC IY	Decrement IY
DEC ss	Decrement Reg. pair ss
DI	Disable interrupts
DJNZ e	Decrement B and Jump relative if B≠0
EI	Enable interrupts
EX (SP),HL	Exchange the location (SP) and HL
EX (SP),IX	Exchange the location (SP) and IX
EX (SP),IY	Exchange the location (SP) and IY
EX AF,AF'	Exchange the contents of AF and AF'
EX DE,HL	Exchange the contents of DE and HL
EXX	Exchange the contents of BC,DE,HL with contents of BC',DE',HL' respectively
HALT	HALT (wait for interrupt or reset)
IM 0	Set interrupt mode 0
IM 1	Set interrupt mode 1
IM 2	Set interrupt mode 2

Mnemonics	Description
IN A,(n)	Load the Acc. with input from device n
IN r,(C)	Load the Reg. r with input from device (C)
INC (HL)	Increment location (HL)
INC IX	Increment IX
INC (IX+d)	Increment location (IX+d)
INC IY	Increment IY
INC (IY+d)	Increment location (IY+d)
INC r	Increment Reg. r
INC ss	Increment Reg. pair ss
IND	Load location (HL) with input from port (C), decrement HL and B
INDR	Load location (HL) with input from port (C), decrement HL and decrement B, repeat until B=0
INI	Load location (HL) with input from port (C); and increment HL and decrement B
INIR	Load location (HL) with input from port (C), increment HL and decrement B, repeat until B=0
JP (HL)	Unconditional Jump to (HL)
JP (IX)	Unconditional Jump to (IX)
JP (IY)	Unconditional Jump to (IY)
JP cc,nn	Jump to location nn if condition cc is true
JP nn	Unconditional jump to location nn
JR C,e	Jump relative to PC+e if carry=1
JR e	Unconditional Jump relative to PC+e
JR NC,e	Jump relative to PC+e if carry=0
JR NZ,e	Jump relative to PC+e if non zero (Z=0)
JR Z,e	Jump relative to PC+e if zero (Z=1)
LD A,(BC)	Load Acc. with location (BC)
LD A,(DE)	Load Acc. with location (DE)
LD A,I	Load Acc. with I
LD A,(nn)	Load Acc. with location nn
LD A,R	Load Acc. with Reg. R
LD (BC),A	Load location (BC) with Acc.
LD (DE),A	Load location (DE) with Acc.
LD (HL),n	Load location (HL) with value n
LD dd,nn	Load Reg. pair dd with value nn
LD dd,(nn)	Load Reg. pair dd with location (nn)
LD HL,(nn)	Load HL with location (nn)
LD (HL),r	Load location (HL) with Reg. r
LD I,A	Load I with Acc.
LD IX,nn	Load IX with value nn
LD IX,(nn)	Load IX with location (nn)
LD (IX+d),n	Load location (IX+d) with value n
LD (IX+d),r	Load location (IX+d) with Reg. r

continued overleaf

TABLE 9.1 (contd.)

Mnemonics	Description
LD IY,nn	Load IY with value nn
LD IY,(nn)	Load IY with location (nn)
LD (IY+d),n	Load location (IY+d) with value n
LD (IY+d),r	Load location (IY+d) with Reg. r
LD (nn),A	Load location (nn) with Acc.
LD (nn),dd	Load location (nn) with Reg. pair dd
LD (nn),HL	Load location (nn) with HL
LD (nn),IX	Load location (nn) with IX
LD (nn),IY	Load location (nn) with IY
LD R,A	Load R with Acc.
LD r,(HL)	Load Reg. r with location (HL)
LD r,(IX+d)	Load Reg. r with location (IX+d)
LD r,(IY+d)	Load Reg. r with location (IY+d)
LD r,n	Load Reg. r with value n
LD r,r'	Load Reg. r with Reg. r'
LD SP,HL	Load SP with HL
LD SP,IX	Load SP with IX
LD SP,IY	Load SP with IY
LDD	Load location (DE) with location (HL), decrement DE,HL and BC
LDDR	Load location (DE) with location (HL), decrement DE,HL and BC; repeat until BC=0
LDI	Load location (DE) with location (HL), increment DE,HL, decrement BC
LDIR	Load location (DE) with location (HL), increment DE,HL, decrement BC and repeat until BC=0
NEG	Negate Acc. (2s complement)
NOP	No operation
OR s	Logical "OR" of operand s and Acc.
OTDR	Load output port (C) with location (HL) decrement HL and B, repeat until B=0
OTIR	Load output port (C) with location (HL), increment HL, decrement B, repeat until B=0
OUT (C),r	Load output port (C) with Reg. r
OUT (n),A	Load output port (n) with Acc.
OUTD	Load output port (C) with location (HL), decrement HL and B
OUTI	Load output port (C) with location (HL), increment HL and decrement B
POP IX	Load IX with top of stack
POP IY	Load IY with top of stack
POP qq	Load Reg. pair qq with top of stack
PUSH IX	Load IX onto stack
PUSH IY	Load IY onto stack
PUSH qq	Load Reg. pair qq onto stack

Mnemonics	Description
RES b,m	Reset Bit b of operand m
RET	Return from subroutine
RET cc	Return from subroutine if condition cc is true
RETI	Return from interrupt
RETN	Return from nonmaskable interrupt
RL m	Rotate left through carry operand m
RLA	Rotate left Acc. through carry
RLC (HL)	Rotate location (HL) left circular
RLC (IX+d)	Rotate location (IX+d) left circular
RLC (IY+d)	Rotate location (IY+d) left circular
RLC r	Rotate Reg. r left circular
RLCA	Rotate left circular Acc.
RLD	Rotate digit left and right between Acc. and location (HL)
RR m	Rotate right through carry operand m
RRA	Rotate right Acc. through carry
RRC m	Rotate operand m right circular
RRCA	Rotate right circular Acc.
RRD	Rotate digit right and left between Acc. and location (HL)
RST p	Restart to location p
SBC A,s	Subtract operand s from Acc. with carry
SBC HL,ss	Subtract Reg. pair ss from HL with carry
SCF	Set carry flag (C=1)
SET B,(HL)	Set Bit b of location (HL)
SET b,(IX+d)	Set Bit b of location (IX+d)
SET b,(IY+d)	Set Bit b of location (IY+d)
SET b,r	Set Bit b of Reg. r
SLA m	Shift operand m left arithmetic
SRA m	Shift operand m right arithmetic
SRL m	Shift operand m right logical
SUB s	Subtract operand s from Acc.
XOR s	Exclusive "OR" operand s and Acc.

It is perhaps unfortunate that although the machine code for all of the 8080 and 8085 instructions is identical with the Z80, the Z80 uses different mnemonics. There are few unused opcodes in the 8080/8085 instruction set, and so the Z80 combines an unused object code byte with a second byte to form a 2-byte opcode for the additional instructions which it offers. Therefore 4-byte instructions (2 bytes for opcode plus 2 bytes for operand) are used frequently by the Z80. These additional instructions offer the following facilities:

(i) A single block move instruction (e.g. LDD) enables a block of data to be moved from one part of memory to another, or even between memory and input/output (e.g. OUTD).

(ii) A block of memory can be scanned (or searched) for a specific value (e.g. CPDR).

(iii) An individual bit in a register or memory location can be examined (e.g. BIT 4,C) or altered (e.g. SET 6,B).

(iv) The second register set can be selected. For example, changeover to the complete second set can be accomplished (typically within an interrupt routine) as follows:

```
EXX                 ;Exchange BC, DE and HL
EX     AF,AF'       ;Exchange AF
```

When these additional features are combined with indexed and program counter relative addressing, it is easy to appreciate the considerable computing power which is offered by the Z80.

9.2 THE ZILOG PIO

The Zilog PIO is a more typical parallel input/output chip than the Intel 8155, which was described in the last chapter. Figure 9.4 shows a generalised diagram of the interconnection between a Z80 CPU and a Z80 PIO. However, in addition to the two programmable ports, the PIO does offer an interrupt handling capability—more of this last feature later. The diagram shows that there are five control bus signal lines connected—$\overline{M1}$, $\overline{IORQ}$, $\overline{RD}$, $\overline{INT}$ and ϕ (same as CPU clock). The two signals $C/\overline{D}$ and $B/\overline{A}$ are used to select one of four addresses on the device, as follows (notice that $C/\overline{D}$ stands for Control/$\overline{Data}$):

$B/\overline{A}$	$C/\overline{D}$	
0	0	Port A data
0	1	Port A control
1	0	Port B data
1	1	Port B control

Thus each of the two ports possesses its own control register. Clearly two lower-order address lines (normally A0 and A1) are connected to these signals.

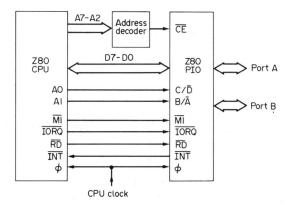

Fig. 9.4. The Zilog PIO.

The bit pattern within each control register is detailed in Fig. 9.5. The bottom four bits must be set to 1111 in order to initialise the port. The top two bits determine the programmable mode of the port. Normally the ports are used in either mode 0 (output) or mode 1 (input). The more complicated modes of operation are to select each pin as either an output or an input signal (mode 3—the following byte output represents pin directions, 1 = input, 0 = output) and to use handshaking between ports and remote logic (mode 2—the handshaking signals STB and RDY are not shown in Fig. 9.4 for simplicity).

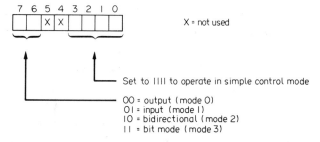

Fig. 9.5. Control register for Z80 PIO.

If the address bus is connected to the device so that the following addresses apply:

20	Port A data
21	Port A control
22	Port B data
23	Port B control

then the following program example could be used to initialise port A as output and port B as input, and then output all 1s to port A:

```
LD    A,0FH      ;Control word for output (mode 0)
OUT   21H,A      ;Output to port A control register
LD    A,4FH      ;Control word for input (mode 1)
OUT   23H,A      ;Output to port B control register
LD    A,FFH      ;Bit pattern of 1111 1111
OUT   20H,A      ;Output to port A
```

Normally a Z80 PIO is used in this manner only. The interrupt line $\overline{\text{INT}}$ is not connected and the device is not used in the interrupt mode. However, the device can be initialised, or programmed, to generate an interrupt when, for example, a specific input bit is set, or it can even generate part of the interrupt vector. Recall the three CPU interrupt modes (which are quite separate from the four PIO operating modes). For example, if the CPU is set by program instruction (IM 2) to operate in interrupt mode 2, then the following program sequence can be used to set the PIO to generate an interrupt vector:

(a) set port to mode 3 (output to control register),
(b) output pin directions,
(c) output interrupt vector byte.

For further details of the initialising procedure for the generation of interrupts, the reader is referred to the data sheets for the device.

9.3 THE ZILOG COUNTER TIMER CIRCUIT (CTC)

Zilog offer another useful CPU support chip. The Z80 CTC is a four-channel counter/timer chip, i.e. it possesses four channels, each of

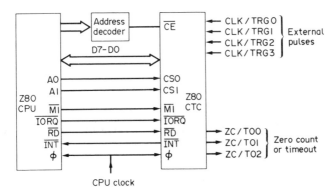

Fig. 9.6. The Zilog CTC (Counter Timer Circuit).

which can be selected as an event counter or an interval timer. In the former application a count is output from the CPU and decremented by pulses which represent external events; an interrupt can be generated when the count reaches zero. In the second application a precise time interval can be generated if a count is output from the CPU and decremented by the system clock; again an interrupt can be generated when the count reaches zero.

The generalised method of interconnection between a Z80 CPU and a Z80 CTC is shown in Fig. 9.6. The interconnections between CPU and CTC are as for the CPU and PIO; the CS0 and CS1 signals are used to select the address of one of the four channels. There are two different sets of external signals as follows:

(a) CLK/TRG—these can be connected from external circuits when it is required to operate a channel in the counter mode

(b) ZC/TO—these are signals which are available to indicate that a count is zero. They are not normally used because indication to the CPU that a count in a channel has reached zero is achieved by the generation of an interrupt on the $\overline{INT}$ line. However, they offer an additional application of the device—that of a pulse generator. If a channel is selected to run as an interval timer then effectively the ZC/TO signal is pulsed every time the count reaches zero, and this signal can be used as a slow clock pulse for any other device or

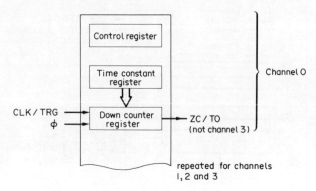

FIG. 9.7. Z80 CTC channel.

circuit in the system. An example of such a device is a UART, and the baud rate can be altered by setting a different clock rate into the UART—the clock pulses are generated on the CTC ZC/TO signal.

Each of the four channels in the Z80 CTC possesses three registers as shown in Fig. 9.7. An initial count is loaded into the Time Constant Register. This count is transferred to the Down Counter Register at the beginning of a counter or timer operation. The Down Counter can be read by the CPU at any time. The Control Register is loaded from the CPU in order to select the programmable options of the channel.

The bit pattern in the Control Register is detailed in Fig. 9.8. Bit 0 must be set to 1 to select control mode. If bit 1 (Reset) is a 0 then every time the Down Counter Register reaches zero it is reloaded automatically from the Time Constant Register and channel operations recommence; if the bit is 1 the channel stops immediately. Bit 2 (Load) is set to a 1 when a time constant, i.e. new count for either counter or timer operation, is to be output; this 8-bit value is sent as a second output operation. Bits 3, 4 and 5 (Trigger, Slope and Range) are self-explanatory. Bit 6 (Mode) is set to 1 to select counter mode and to 0 to select timer mode. Bit 7 (Interrupt Enable) enables or disables the channel's interrupt logic. If it is required to operate the CPU in interrupt mode 2 and to generate an interrupt vector from the CTC, then the vector must be initialised into the CTC by an output operation (to channel 0) which has bit 0 set to 0 and the other bits set to the vector address.

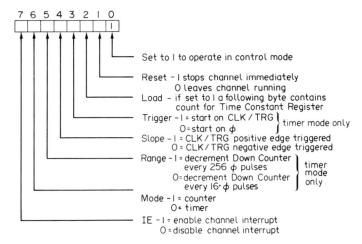

FIG. 9.8. Control register for Z80 CTC.

The following program example initialises a Z80 CTC (addresses hex. 10, 11, 12 and 13 for channels 0, 1, 2 and 3) as follows:

(1) Channel 0 as a timer, with a time constant of hex. 40 and an interrupt vector (start address of servicing routine) of hex. 3080.
(2) Channel 1 as a counter, with a time constant of hex. 100 and an interrupt vector of hex. 3082.
(3) Channel 2 as a frequency divider, e.g. a clock generator for a UART, with a time constant of decimal 104.
(4) Channel 3—not used.

```
;Set interrupt vector
IM      2             ;Set CPU to interrupt mode 2
LD      A,30H         ;Top half of interrupt vector
LD      I,A           ;Load into Interrupt Register
LD      A,80H         ;Bottom half of interrupt vector
OUT     (10H),A       ;Output to CTC
;Initialise channel 0 as timer
LD      A,A5H         ;Control code
OUT     (10H),A       ;Output to channel 0
LD      A,40H         ;Time constant
```

```
OUT  (10H),A     ;Output to channel 0
;Initialise channel 1 as counter
LD    A,D5H      ;Control code
OUT  (11H),A     ;Output to channel 1
LD    A,100H     ;Time constant
OUT  (11H),A     ;Output to channel 1
;Initialise channel 2 as clock generator for UART
LD    A,05H      ;Control code
OUT  (12H),A     ;Output to channel 2
LD    A,104H     ;Time constant
OUT  (12H),A     ;Output to channel 2
```

The reader may like to calculate the time delay from channel 0 and the baud rate of the UART (assume that an 8251A USART—see Section 8.3—is used with a baud rate factor of x1) if the clock rate is 2 MHz. Answers are given at the end of the chapter.

9.4 EXAMPLES

(a) Reading a Group of Contact Closures

Assume that the Z80 PIO port of Fig. 9.9 is initialised to operate as an input port, and its address is hex. 40. Four manual pushbuttons are connected to the port. The following program reads the port and if the pushbutton on the second signal pin only is closed (indicated by a 1) then a 1 is set on the least significant bit of an output port at address hex. 42.

```
          IN    A,(40H)       ;Input from port to accumulator
          AND   2             ;Mask all bits except second
          JR    Z,CLOSED      ;Jump if second bit is set to 1
          JR    END           ;Unconditional jump to end of
                                 program
CLOSED:LD       A,1           ;Load accumulator with 1
          OUT   (42H),A       :Output to output port, e.g. to
                                 light LED
     END:HALT                 ;Halt
```

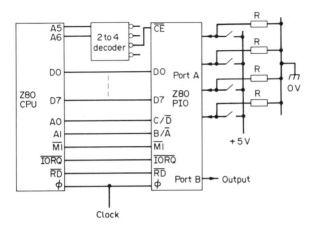

FIG. 9.9. Z80 Example—group of contact closures.

(b) Reading a Multiplexed Analogue Input System

Assume the hardware arrangement of Fig. 9.10. A Z80 PIO is connected to an 8-bit A/D converter (ZN 427E) via port B. Three signals on port A are used as handshaking signals to control the A/D. Additionally four output signals on port A are connected to an analogue multiplexor IC (CD 4051 BE). Whichever code is set on these four bits selects one of eight analogue signals. The selected analogue signal passes through to the A/D chip for conversion.

The address of the two ports are:

Port A data   = hex. 06
Port A control = hex. 16
Port B data   = hex. 26
Port B control = hex. 36

The following program section initialises the two ports to the required directions:

```
LD    A,CFH      ;Set port A to individual
OUT   (16H),A    ;                    bit mode (mode 3)
```

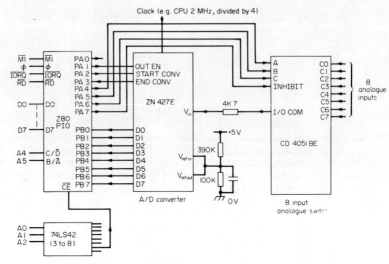

FIG. 9.10. Multiplexed 8-channel analogue input system for Z80
(courtesy M. D. Truman).

```
LD      A,08H       ;Set PA3 to input and
OUT     (16),A      ;                       PAO–PA7 to output
                                                (excluding PA3)
LD      A,CFH       ;Set port B to individual
OUT     (36H),A     ;                       bit mode (mode 3)
LD      A,FFH       ;Set all bits
OUT     (36H),A     ;           to input
```

The reader may like to examine a shorter method of initialising port B as
input using mode 1.

The following program section selects the third analogue input, passes
it through the A/D converter and reads in the digital value:

```
        LD      A,2         ;Select third analogue input
        OUT     (06H),A     ;Output to analogue switch (multiplexor)
        ADD     A,6         ;Set OUT EN and START CONV bits
        OUT     (06H),A     ;Output to A/D
POLL:IN         A,(06H)     ;Input from port A
```

```
BIT   3,A          ;Check END CONV bit
JR    Z,POLL       ;Poll this bit until set to 1
IN    (26H),A      ;Input A/D count
```

(*Answers*: 8.192 msec and 1200 baud.)

BIBLIOGRAPHY

1. *An Introduction to Microcomputers*, Vol. 2. A. Osborne. Osborne, 1978.
2. *Z80 Assembly Language Programming*. Lance C. Leventhel. Osborne, 1979.
3. *Z80 Microcomputer Handbook*. William Barden, Jr. Prentice-Hall, 1978.
4. *Z80 Microprocessor Programming and Interfacing*—Books 1 and 2. Elizabeth A. Nichols, Joseph C. Nichols and Peter R. Rony. Prentice-Hall, 1979.

CHAPTER 10

Interfacing the Texas Instruments 9980A Microprocessor

10.1 THE 9980A MICROPROCESSOR

In the late 1970s Texas Instruments decided not to enter the over-subscribed 8-bit market, which was filled with the 8080, 8085, Z80, 6800 and 6502 microprocessors, but were the first manufacturer to mass produce a 16-bit microprocessor. Their 9900 range of microprocessors are really minicomputers designed onto single chips.

The 9980A has no on-chip registers (or accumulators); they are held in RAM. Thus it is slower than the 16-bit microprocessors which have been introduced by other manufacturers, e.g. the 8086, Z8000, 68000 and 16000, because each instruction which utilises a work register must perform a memory (RAM) transfer. Also it has the most limited addressing range—14 address lines in place of the normal 16 lines—although an alternative CPU in the range (the 9900) does offer the full 16 lines. However, it possesses an extremely powerful interrupt handling capability. When an interrupt occurs it is not necessary to store the contents of registers in memory (they are already there), and the CPU simply switches to a new set of 16 registers elsewhere in memory.

As a result of good marketing the 9900 series CPUs are widely used in a variety of applications, e.g. industrial sequence controllers (PLCs—programmable logic controllers), fruit (gaming) machines, cash registers.

The 9980A microprocessor has a 16K addressing range and its 16 registers are any consecutive 16 words in RAM. All of its registers are effectively accumulators, i.e. the results of ALU operations can be placed

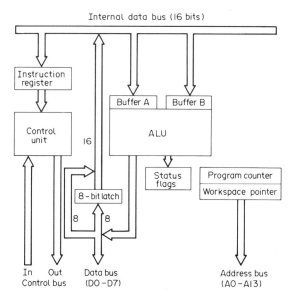

Fig. 10.1. The Texas Instruments 9980A microprocessor.

in any register. It possesses four prioritised interrupts. It is held in a 40-pin package.

Figure 10.1 shows the internal organisation of the CPU. The 8-bit latch is necessary with some 16-bit microprocessors if the external data bus is only 8 bits. Consequently 2 bytes of memory have to be transferred for each 16-bit memory transfer, and these are placed in parallel for the internal 16-bit bus of the CPU. Clearly the ALU and instruction register are 16 bits in operation. The program counter is only 14 bits long to handle the 14-line address bus; note how Texas Instruments (TI) number their address and data buses in reverse order to Intel, Zilog and others. The contents of the program counter are updated automatically by 2, 4 or 6 at the end of each instruction for 1, 2 or 3 word instructions respectively (remember that one 16-bit word equals two memory bytes or locations). The workspace pointer indicates the start address in RAM of the 16 registers.

MI-F

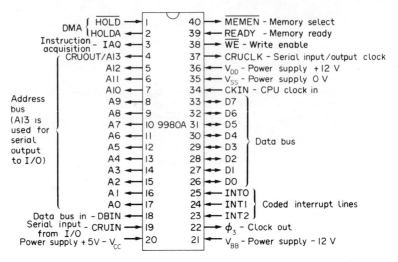

FIG. 10.2. 9980A pin connections.

This 16-bit CPU offers 16-bit arithmetic. Therefore the number range is approximately $-32,000$ to $+32,000$, which is an enormous improvement over an 8-bit CPU (256 numbers only). Multiplication and division instructions are available, as well as multi-bit shift instructions.

Figure 10.2 shows the pin connections. The reader may notice the commonality between many of the signals on the Intel 8085 and the TI device, e.g. IO/$\overline{M}$ (Intel) equates to $\overline{MEMEN}$ (TI), the $\overline{RD}$ and $\overline{WR}$ functions (Intel) are served by $\overline{WE}$ (TI), etc. One unusual feature of the 9980A is that data is *not* transferred between CPU and input/output (e.g. PIOs and UARTs) using the data bus. Instead a serial input line (CRUIN) and a serial output line (CRUOUT) plus a synchronising clock (CRUCLK) are used. This has the effect of reducing the number of pin connections from 8 (data bus) to 3 (serial lines plus clock) on an input/output IC.

The instruction set for the 9900 series of microprocessors is shown in Table 10.1. The addressing modes which are available are shown on p. 153 ($>$ denotes hex.).

TABLE 10.1 TEXAS INSTRUMENTS 9980A INSTRUCTION SET

Mnemonic	Description

(a) *Move*
MOVE, LOAD and STORE

LI Rn,IOP	Load register n with immediate operand
LWPI IOP	Load workspace pointer with immediate operand
MOV S,D	Move from S (source) to D (destination)
MOVB S,D	Move from S (source) to D (destination)—byte operation
STST Rn	Store status register in register n
STWP Rn	Store workspace pointer in register n

INPUT/OUTPUT

LDCR Rn,N	Output N bits from register n
STCR Rn,N	Input N bits to register n
SBO N	Set single bit output to 1 (N bits displacement)
SBZ N	Set single bit output to 0 (N bits displacement)
TB N	Input single input/output bit (N bits displacement)

(b) *Modify*
INCREMENT/DECREMENT

INC S	Increment source
INCT S	Increment source by 2
DEC S	Decrement source
DECT S	Decrement source by 2

ARITHMETIC

A S,D	Add source to destination
AI Rn,IOP	Add immediate operand to register n
S S,D	Subtract source from destination
SB S,D	Subtract source from destination—byte operation
MPY S,Rn	Multiply source by register n
DIV S,Rn	Divide source by register n

LOGICAL

ANDI Rn,IOP	AND immediate operand with register n
ORI Rn,IOP	OR immediate operand with register n
XOR S,Rn	EXCLUSIVE OR source with register n
CI Rn,IOP	Compare immediate operand with register n
COC S,Rn	Compare ones corresponding source with register n
CZC S,Rn	Compare zeros corresponding source with register n
C S,D	Compare source with destination
CB S,D	Compare source with destination—byte operation
SOC S,D	Set ones corresponding
SOCB S,D	Set ones corresponding—byte operation
SZC S,D	Set zeros corresponding
SZCB S,D	Set zeros corresponding—byte operation
SETO S	Set to ones source

SHIFT/ROTATE

SLA Rn,N	Shift left (arithmetic) N bits
SRA Rn,N	Shift right (arithmetic) N bits

continued overleaf

TABLE 10.1 (contd.)

Mnemonic	Description
SRL Rn,N	Shift right (logical) N bits
SRC Rn,N	Shift right (cyclical) N bits
SPECIALS	
INV S	Invert source
NEG S	Negate source
ABS S	Absolute value source
(c) *JUMP*	
JUMP	
JMP DISP	Unconditional jump
JLT DISP	Jump if less than
JLE DISP	Jump if low or equal
JEQ DISP	Jump if equal
JHE DISP	Jump if high or equal
JGT DISP	Jump if greater than
JNE DISP	Jump if not equal
JNC DISP	Jump if no carry
JOC DISP	Jump if carry
JNO DISP	Jump if no overflow
JL DISP	Jump if low
JH DISP	Jump if high
JOP DISP	Jump if odd parity
Note: DISP (displacement) can be positive or negative	
B D	Branch (jump) to address D
(d) *Subroutine*	
CALL	
BL D	Branch and link to address D
BLWP D	Branch and link to address D and change WP
RETURN	
RTWP	Return to main program with old WP
(e) *Interrupts and Control*	
INTERRUPTS	
LIMI	Load immediate interrupt mask
CONTROL	
IDLE	Suspend program operation
RSET	Reset
CKOF	User defined
CKON	User defined
LREX	User defined
XOP	Extended operation
X	Execute

S (source) and D (destination) can be any register or any memory location in a variety of addressing modes.

(a) Register Direct Addressing

e.g.   MOV R1,R4

moves the contents of register 1 to register 4.

(b) Register Indirect Addressing

e.g.   MOV R3,*R6

moves the contents of register 3 to the memory address which is held in register 6.

(c) Register Indirect Addressing, Autoincrement Register

e.g.   MOV R2,*R8+

moves the contents of register 2 to the memory address which is held in register 8, and increments the address in register 8 by 2 (thus register 8 points to the next 16-bit word address in memory).

(d) Symbolic Memory Addressing, not Indexed

e.g.   MOV R4,@>3F00

moves the contents of register 4 to the memory address 3F00. This instruction is a two-word instruction therefore because the address 3F00 is held in the second 16-bit word of the instruction.

(e) Symbolic Memory Addressing, Indexed

e.g.   MOV R7,@>0500(R2)

moves the contents of register 7 to the memory address 0500 *plus* the contents of register 2. For example, if register 2 contains 6, then the destination is 0506.

(f) Immediate Addressing

e.g.   LI R3,9

moves the number 9 into register 3. Clearly this is a two-word instruction, with the number 9 held in the second 16-bit word.

(g) Absolute Memory Addressing (for transferring program control)

e.g.   B   @>2000

branches, or jumps unconditionally, to the program instruction at memory location 2000.

(h) Relative Addressing

e.g.   JGT +5

jumps (if greater than) forward 5 16-bit words,

or   JLT −25

jumps (if less than) back 23 16-bit words.

Consider the following program, which adds 8 numbers which are loaded in memory starting at hex. 4000:

```
          LWPI  >300        ;Set workspace pointer to hex. 0300
          LI    R1,>4000    ;Load register 1 with 4000
          LI    R2,0        ;Clear register 2
          LI    R3,8        ;Loop count in register 3
REPEAT:A        *R1+,R2     ;Add from memory into register 2
          DEC   R3          ;Decrement loop count
          JGT   REPEAT      ;Repeat (total of 8 times)
          MOV   R2,R9       ;Move answer to register 9
  HERE:JMP      HERE        ;Loop stop
```

The reader may like to compare this program with a similar example program which is given for the Intel 8085 in section 8.1. The programs are virtually identical, except that the 9980A program requires an initial LWPI instruction to specify the start location in memory of the 16 registers, whilst it requires one less instruction because its autoincrement addressing mode in the A (add) instruction replaces the Intel INX instruction.

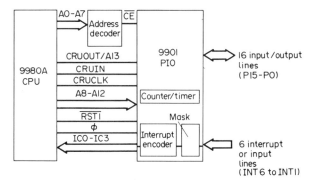

FIG. 10.3. The TI 9901 PIO.

10.2 THE TEXAS INSTRUMENTS 9901 PIO

The TI 9901 PIO chip, which is illustrated in Fig. 10.3, offers the following facilities:

(a) 16 input/output lines,
(b) 6 interrupt/input lines,
(c) counter/timer.

The number of input/output signals (22) is the same as for the Intel 8155 PIO. However, the final 6 signals can be selected to act as either normal input lines or as interrupts. In the latter case the setting of a particular interrupt line $\overline{INT6}$ to $\overline{INT1}$ causes the PIO to present a code on the control bus interrupt lines IC0 to IC3. An internal mask exists in the 9901, and the programmer can set the 6 lines as inputs rather than interrupts by setting this mask to prevent processing of these signals as interrupts. In fact the number of external interrupt lines can be extended from 6 to 15 if additionally the input/output signals P15 to P7 are set to act as interrupts also.

After reset all input/output signals are programmed as inputs. Writing to an output signal sets that line as an output. Before we examine the techniques for initialising a 9901 by software to predefine the roles of its 22 input/output signals, we must first examine the technique for transfer-

ring data between CPU and input/output devices. Two instructions are
used as follows:

```
LI      R12,>100        ;Set input/output address of hex. 100
LDCR  R3,11             ;Output eleven bits from register 3
```

The output instruction LDCR specifies the data which is to be transferred
only (contents of register 3); it does not include an input/output address.
This address must be set in register 12 previously, because the contents of
register 12 are set on the address bus whenever an input or output
instruction is implemented.

Five address lines are connected to the 9901. Therefore, there are 32
separate addresses on the device, allowing discrete addressing of each
input/output signal. The last 16 bit addresses are the signal lines P0 to P15,
whilst the first bit address is the control bit. The remaining 15 bits are used
to define the 15 possible interrupt lines as interrupts or input/output
signals, and also they carry the count values to/from the counter/timer.

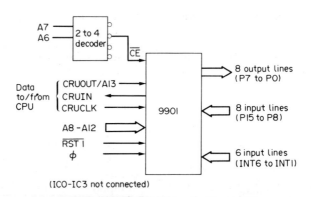

(ICO–IC3 not connected)

Fig. 10.4. Typical 9901 input/output configuration.

A possible configuration of the 9901 is shown in Fig. 10.4. The method
of initialising the device to this particular arrangement is as follows:

```
LI      R12,>40         ;Input/output address of 9901
CLR     R3              ;Clear register 3
LDCR  R3,7              ;Output seven 0s to control bit and six INT
```

```
                    ;   lines—sets INT lines as input, not
                        interrupts
LI      R12,>60     ;Input/output address of P7 to P0
LDCR    R3,8        ;Set P7 to P0 as outputs (output from R3)
LI      R12,>70     ;Input/output address of P15 to P8
STCR    R4,8        ;Set P15 to P8 as inputs (input to R4)
```

The reader may have expected an address range of hex. 40 to hex. 5F in order to cover the 32 bit addresses. However, the address range is hex. 40 to hex. 7E because A13 (least significant address line) is not connected to the device as an address line—it is used to carry the data in serial form from the CPU to the 9901 during an output instruction (along CRUOUT). Therefore, bit addresses, which are set in register 12, increment by 2.

The following three program sections perform the same function, i.e. set the third pin on a 9901 to logic 1:

```
(1) LI      R12,>420    ;Input/output address hex. 420
    LI      R6,8        ;Set bit pattern 0000 0000 0000 1000
    LDCR    R6,0        ;Output 16 bits from register 6
```
(The 0 in this last instruction means transfer the full 16 bits.)

```
(2) LI      R12,>420    ;Input/output address hex. 420
    SBO     3           ;Output a 1 to third pin down
```
(The 3 in the last instruction represents a bit displacement from the address in register 12.)

```
(3) LI      R12,>426    ;Input/output address hex. 426
    SBO     0           ;Output a 1 to same pin
```

The counter/timer circuit on the 9901 can be initialised to produce a delay of up to approximately 0.25 sec. Alternatively it can generate timing interrupt pulses at the same rate.

A program section which generates a fixed 0.2 sec delay is as follows:

```
        LIMI    0       ;Disable interrupts (set interrupt
                            mask in CPU)
        LI      R12,>40 ;Input/output address of 9901
        SBZ     0       ;Set control bit to zero (enter
                            interrupt mode)
        SBO     3       ;Clear clock interrupt
```

```
        LI      R4,>30D5        ;Delay count for 0.2 sec
        LDCR    R4,0            ;Output to counter/timer
POLL:TB         15              ;Input count complete bit
        JNE     POLL            ;Poll this bit
```

The program continues past the last instruction after precisely 0.2 sec (if the CPU clock is 8 MHz).

Alternatively if the program is to set the counter/timer to generate an interrupt when the count reaches zero, the following program can be used:

```
LI      R12,>40     ;Input/output address of 9901
SBZ     0           ;Set control bit to zero (enter interrupt mode)
SBO     3           ;Clear clock interrupt
LI      R4,>30D5    ;Delay count for 0.2 sec
LDCR    R4,0        ;Output to counter/timer
LIMI    1           ;Enable all interrupts
```

In this case the count complete condition causes the counter/timer to generate an interrupt. If this interrupt is on interrupt level 1 then the appropriate vector must be set in memory to direct entry into the servicing interrupt routine. In fact the 9980A requires two vectors for each interrupt; memory locations 0004 and 0006 must contain the WP vector (new workspace pointer for the interrupt routine) and the PC vector (the program counter setting for the interrupt routine, i.e. the start address) for this particular interrupt.

10.3 THE TEXAS INSTRUMENTS 9902 UART

The Texas Instruments 9902 UART is a programmable device which can interface with any of the 9900 range of CPUs and provide a serial asynchronous channel. Additionally it offers a completely separate counter/timer facility.

The interconnection signals are shown in Fig. 10.5. The clock pulses are required to trigger the serial data transfer; they are divided internally to generate the required baud rate.

The INT interrupt signal is available to indicate the count complete state on the counter/timer.

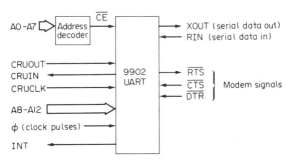

FIG. 10.5. The TI 9902 UART.

The external modem signals are shown. Commonly $\overline{RTS}$ and $\overline{CTS}$ are connected together.

There are 32 addresses on the chip to handle data output and input, as well as a control register which is used to program, or initialise, the device. It is not appropriate to define all bit identities and device options here; that information can be obtained from the manufacturer's data sheets. However, Fig. 10.6 shows the identities of the individual bits in the control register. Notice that the only flexibility in terms of varying the baud rate in the control register is by means of the "divide by 3" bit.

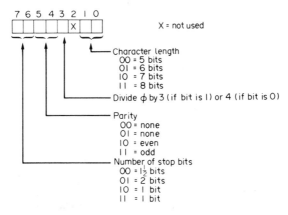

FIG. 10.6. Control register for 9902 UART.

However, the 9902, unlike the Intel 8251A, offers a baud rate setting which is fully programmable over the whole range of normal speeds (e.g. 110, 300, 600, etc.). This is achieved by outputting a further initialising byte to the device, as demonstrated in the following program:

```
LI      R12,>80         ;Input/output address of 9902
SBO  31                 ;Reset UART command
LI      R1,>A200        ;Output parity, stop
LDCR  R1,8             ;                         bits, character length
LI      R1,>1A1         ;Output receive
LDCR  R1,11            ;                        baud rate (110)
LI      R1,>4D0         ;Output transmit
LDCR  R1,12            ;                        baud rate (300)
```

The device is then fully initialised to transmit at 300 baud and receive at 110 baud. The values hex. 1A1 and hex. 4D0 are calculated as multiples of the incoming clock rate (1 MHz).

The following program transmits a character (the ASCII for the letter W) and then enters a wait loop until the UART has completed transmission:

```
        LI      R12,>80         ;Input/output address of 9902
        SBO  16                 ;Turn on transmitter
        LI      R4,>5700        ;ASCII for letter W
        LDCR  R4,8             ;Output top 8 bits from register 4
POLL:TB     22                 ;Wait until transmit
        JNE    POLL            ;                         buffer is empty
```

Conversely the following program enters a wait loop until a character is received, and then passes this character into register 5:

```
        LI      R12,>80         ;Input/output address of 9902
POLL:TB     21                 ;Wait until receive
        JNE    POLL            ;                         buffer is empty
        STCR  R5,8             ;Input 8-bit character to register 5
        SBZ   18                 ;Reset receive buffer full marker
```

10.4 EXAMPLES

(a) Lighting a LED

The following program lights one of two LEDs, which are connected to adjacent signal pins on a 9901 at input/output address hex. 20, depending on the result of a comparison between the contents of two memory locations:

```
        LWPI  >0300              ;Set workspace pointer
        C     @>340,@>342        ;Compare contents of memory
                                    locations
        JEQ   SAME               ;Jump if same
        LI    R12,>20            ;Set address of LED1
        JMP   LIGHT              ;Jump
SAME:LI       R12,>22            ;Set address of LED2
LIGHT:SBO     0                  ;Output 1 to one of the LEDs
  END:JMP     END                ;Stop
```

(b) Driving a Stepper Motor

The following program rotates a stepper motor by one revolution in a clockwise direction:

```
        LWPI  >300               ;Set workspace pointer
        LI    R12,>20            ;Input/output address
        LI    R1,48              ;Loop count (48 pulses per revolution)
        SBO   1                  ;Output 1 for direction clockwise
  LOOP:SBO    0                  ;Output a 1 for leading edge of pulse
        BL    @DELAY             ;Delay (1 msec)
        SBZ   0                  ;Output a 0 for trailing edge of pulse
        BL    @DELAY             ;Delay (1 msec)
        DEC   R1                 ;Decrement loop count (number of
                                    pulses)
        JGT   LOOP               ;Repeat (total of 48 pulses)
  HERE:JMP    HERE               ;Stop on this instruction
DELAY:LI      R2,90              ;Delay loop count (start of subroutine)
PAUSE:DEC     R2                 ;Count down
```

```
      JGT   PAUSE        ;                delay count (total of
                                              1 msec)
      B     *R11         ;Return to main program
```

The delay is held in a subroutine DELAY.

(c) Driving a Segment Display

Examine the circuit of Fig. 10.7. The monostable multivibrator must be repeatedly pulsed in order to allow the segment pattern to pass through the gates to drive the LED segments. The following program displays the numbers 1, 2, 3 and 4 on the left-hand four display units:

```
        LWPI  >300        :Set workspace pointer
        LI    R12,>420    ;Input/output address
START:  LI    R1,>360     ;Start address of data table in memory
        LI    R2,4        ;Loop count (4 digits)
LOOP:   MOV   *R1+,R3     ;Move value from data table to
                              register 3
        LDCR  R3,0        ;Output 16 bits from register 3
        SBZ   12          ;Set DISPLAYTRIGGER to 0
        DEC   R2          ;Decrement loop count
        JGT   LOOP        ;Repeat (total of 4 times)
        JMP   START       ;Repeat entire program
```

The following data table must be established at memory location 360:

Memory location	pgfe dcba	Contents (hex.)
360	0001 1111 1001 0000	1F90
362	0001 1010 0100 0001	1A41
364	0001 1011 0000 0010	1B02
366	0001 1001 1001 0011	1993

```
                  ↑     ‾‾‾‾‾‾‾  ‾‾‾‾
DISPLAYTRIGGER          8        4
                     segments  digit
                     (inverse  select
                     logic)
```

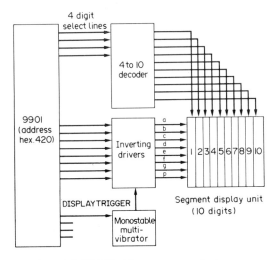

Fig. 10.7. TI 9901 drive to segment display.

(d) Driving a D/A Converter

The straightforward circuit of Fig 10.8 uses an 8-bit D/A converter followed by a 741 op-amp (or its variation the 72741) to generate an analogue voltage of variable range. The signal could feed a graph plotter, pen recorder, servo (position controller), etc.

The following program generates a staircase waveform on the output connection:

```
        LWPI   >300        ;Set workspace pointer
        LI     R12,>20     ;Input/output address
START:  LI     R1,8        ;Loop count (8 steps in staircase)
        LI     R2,0        ;Clear register 2
LOOP:   LDCR   R2,0        ;Output register 2 contents to D/A
        AI     R2,32       :Increase register 2
        LI     R3,100      ;Program
DELAY:  DEC    R3          ;          delay
        JGT    DELAY       ;              loop
        DEC    R1          ;Decrement loop count
```

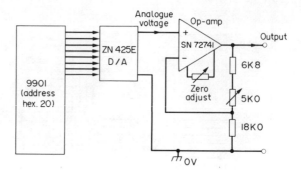

FIG. 10.8. TI 9901 drive to D/A converter.

JGT	LOOP	;Repeat (total of 8 times)—1 staircase
JMP	START	;Repeat entire program

This test waveform can be applied to a CRO in order to check for linear operation of the D/A. If a much longer delay is inserted it could be applied to a pen recorder for the same purpose.

BIBLIOGRAPHY

1. *Microcomputer Board Manual.* RS Components Ltd, 1982.
2. *Microcomputers for Process Control.* R. C. Holland. Pergamon, 1983.

CHAPTER 11

Interfacing Personal Computers

11.1 THE APPLE II MICROCOMPUTER

A "personal computer" is a microcomputer which is desk-mounted and offers a single-user operator program entry and program run facilities. A CRT (in the form of a TV monitor or a VDU) and a keyboard provide operator interface facilities, and a wide variety of business, scientific, educational and games programs can be implemented.

The Apple II is one of the most common personal computers, and Fig. 11.1 shows the principal hardware components. Direct video drive to a modified domestic television is applied, and a single (128K bytes) or double floppy disk drive is connected. Parallel connection to a printer is available.

The machine offers colour graphics facilities, and it is supported by a range of software packages for office applications, e.g. stock control, sales/general ledger, mailing list, word processor (provides a typist with flexible letter/report entry and modification facilities), etc. Scientific applications in particular can exploit the colour graphics feature, and include histogram display, process mimic display, mathematical function display, simple CAD (computer aided design), etc. Educational applications include CAL (computer assisted learning) programs for use in schools. Games, which are available, are an anathema to the serious computer user, and will not be described here!

The main circuit board supports an MOS Technology 6502 microprocessor and 14 K of ROM and 48 K of RAM. A BASIC interpreter is the standard high level language, although PASCAL can be utilised if an additional board is inserted.

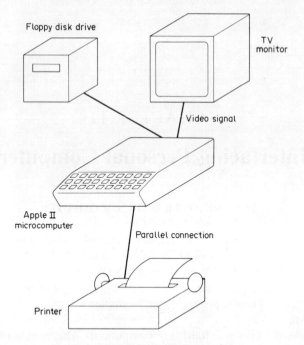

Floppy disk drive

TV monitor

Video signal

Apple II microcomputer

Parallel connection

Printer

FIG. 11.1 Apple II microcomputer system.

Figure 11.2 shows a memory map for the system. The first 2 K of reserved data includes the stack, interrupt vectors and data required for text (non-graphics) and low resolution graphics displays. The user's program, normally in BASIC, is entered into the next 6 K.

The following 16 K supports the area of RAM which holds the memory mapped video data. Two pages of high resolution graphics data are stored, so that fast switching from one display format to the other can be implemented.

Following this area, $13\frac{1}{2}$ K of memory is provided for holding data values and data lists. Apple are often criticised for reserving such an extravagant area for data and such a small area (6 K) for program. A large BASIC program sometimes has to be "overlayed" in this latter area, i.e. one half is loaded from floppy disk first, and when run to completion this

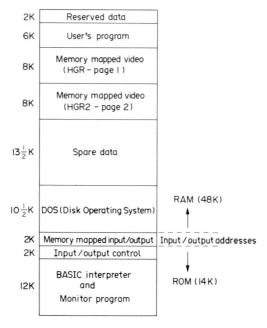

2K	Reserved data
6K	User's program
8K	Memory mapped video (HGR – page I)
8K	Memory mapped video (HGR2 – page 2)
$13\frac{1}{2}$ K	Spare data
$10\frac{1}{2}$ K	DOS (Disk Operating System)
2K	Memory mapped input/output
2K	Input/output control
12K	BASIC interpreter and Monitor program

RAM (48K)

Input/output addresses

ROM (14K)

FIG. 11.2. Apple II memory map.

section calls the second half from disk to be loaded and run on top of the first part.

The operating system DOS (Disk Operating System) fills the last $10\frac{1}{2}$ K of the 48 K of RAM. DOS organises disk transfers and the execution of operator commands.

The next 2 K in the addressing range is not RAM or ROM memory at all. It contains the memory mapped input/output addresses. These are described later.

The final 12 K of ROM provides the BASIC interpreter as well as the monitor program. The latter can be called to allow entry of data values, e.g. to the $13\frac{1}{2}$ K spare data area in RAM.

In text mode a program can utilise the CRT screen to display 24 rows of 40 characters. In high resolution graphics mode (HGR2) the screen is divided into a matrix of 280 (horizontal) and 192 (vertical) plotting points.

Address	Signal identity
49152	Keyboard
49200	Loudspeaker
49240	Bit 0 off ⎫
49241	on ⎪
49242	Bit 1 off ⎪
49243	on ⎬ Digital outputs
49244	Bit 2 off ⎪
49245	on ⎪
49246	Bit 3 off ⎪
49247	on ⎭
49249	Bit 0 ⎫
49250	Bit 1 ⎬ Digital inputs
49251	Bit 2 ⎭
49252	Channel 0 ⎫
49253	1 ⎪ Analogue inputs
49254	2 ⎬ (low quality)
49255	3 ⎭
49264	Reset analogue inputs (low quality)

Add-on analogue input and output board (e.g. slot 2):

49313	Channel 1 ⎫
49314	2 ⎪ Analogue inputs
I	I ⎬ (high quality)
I	I ⎪ and analogue outputs
49329	16 ⎭
49330	⎫
I	⎬ Slot 3
49346	⎭
	etc. (up to slot 7)

FIG. 11.3. Apple II memory mapped input/output addresses.

Lines in 1 of 8 colours can be drawn between any of these points. If some text is to be added to a graphics display, then the matrix can be reduced to 280 × 160 using the HGR option and 4 lines of text can be inserted at the bottom of the display. If it is required to insert text within a graphics screen, the characters must be drawn as shapes. If these shapes are inserted into a "shape table" in the spare data area in RAM, they can be called within a graphics section of program using special Apple graphics commands, e.g.

DRAW 23 AT 85,150

draws shape number 23 (perhaps a letter X or a number 8) at screen position 85 (horizontal), 150 (vertical).

Standard BASIC programming is beyond the scope of this text and is covered in a large number of books—an introduction was given in section

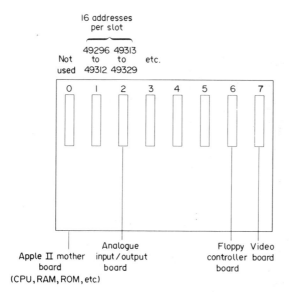

16 addresses
per slot

49296 49313
Not   to   to   etc.
used   49312 49329

0   1   2   3   4   5   6   7

Apple II mother   Analogue   Floppy Video
board   input / output   controller board
(CPU, RAM, ROM, etc.)   board   board

Fig. 11.4. Typical Apple II board assembly (plan view).

7.2. The Apple version, Applesoft BASIC, is described similarly in the manuals which support the Apple machine. The principal features which should be emphasised here are the features which handle input/output operations.

Figure 11.3 lists the input/output addresses which are applied on an Apple II. The first addresses in this memory mapped list represent the keyboard and loudspeaker. Following this are four digital outputs and three digital inputs. Finally four analogue input signals are available. These are low quality signals which are generated from timing circuits and are adjusted by means of variable potentiometers ("pots"). They are intended for use as "paddle" inputs, i.e. manually-adjusted pots for games control. If external analogue input signals, e.g. from an amplified temperature transducer, are to be connected then an add-on board must be inserted. The Apple II "mother board" contains slots into which additional boards can be inserted.

Figure 11.4 shows a typical arrangement of circuit boards. The video board and floppy disk controller board are essential modules in the configuration, but the additional analogue input/output board in slot 2 is arbitrary. It could be inserted in any other vacant slot, except slot 0, which is normally reserved for the video board. Each slot is assigned 16 addresses in the memory mapped input/output area. For example, if 16 analogue inputs are included on this board, e.g. the Mountain Hardware Analogue Board, then each analogue signal possesses 1 of the 16 addresses.

In BASIC the PEEK and POKE commands are used to read from and write to memory respectively. If input/output is memory mapped then the same commands are used to input and output data.

EXAMPLE

Assume that a 16-channel analogue input board is inserted into slot 2. The following Applesoft BASIC program reads the analogue value and displays it in text form:

```
10 REM TEST PROGRAM TO READ ANALOGUE VALUE
20 REM SELECT TEXT MODE, NOT GRAPHICS
30 TEXT
40 REM INPUT A/D COUNT
50 PEEK 49313, COUNT
60 REM DISPLAY A/D COUNT
70 PRINT COUNT
80 END
```

The REM, or comment lines, are non-executable and help the programmer to understand the program listing. The program displays on the CRT the A/D count. If it is required to display the analogue reading in engineering units, e.g. pressure in bar, flow in litres/hour, etc., then the following program can be used:

```
10 REM IMPROVED VERSION, DISPLAYS ENGINEERING UNITS
20 TEXT
30 LRANGE=50
40 HRANGE=250
50 PEEK 49313, COUNT
60 ENGUNITS=COUNT*(HRANGE-LRANGE)/256+LRANGE
70 PRINT ENGUNITS;"DEGC"
80 END
```

for a temperature signal which possesses a range of 50 to 250 degrees C, and an 8-bit A/D (i.e. resolution of 1 in 256). The program displays, for example:

175 DEGC

for an A/D count of 160.

A useful feature with the Apple II is that a 256-byte "page" of ROM is reserved for each input/output board. This gives a total 2 K area of ROM and EPROM (refer to the memory map of Fig. 11.2) for input/output or peripheral control, i.e. a drive program or subroutine can be reserved at the appropriate 256-byte block of memory for each peripheral card.

A wide range of additional peripheral boards are offered by Apple and other manufacturers, e.g. graphics tablet, speech synthesiser.

An extension to a single Apple II system is available so that two or more machines can be interconnected. Thus a "network" of machines can be established. This gives advantages of saving printers, floppy disk units, etc., and also allows one computer to pass data to another. More will be said about such networks in section 11.2.

11.2 THE BBC MICROCOMPUTER

The BBC Model B microcomputer entered the £300 to £800 colour graphics machine market after the Apple II and it offers a similar range of software and hardware facilities. It has obtained wide acceptance for training purposes in educational establishments. Model B offers 32 K of RAM, whilst Model A offers only 16 K. The physical appearance of the BBC is very similar to that of the Apple (see Fig. 11.1).

Initially the BBC machine offered only magnetic tape cassette for back-up storage, but a floppy disk unit was added later. The computer is based on the 6502 microprocessor, like the Apple II and Commodore PET machines. Although the facilities and computing power of this particular chip are often denigrated it still dominates the personal computing market. Its principal rival is the Intel 8088, which is a 16-bit microprocessor and is offered in the ACT Sirius 1 and the IBM personal computer, but these machines are much more expensive.

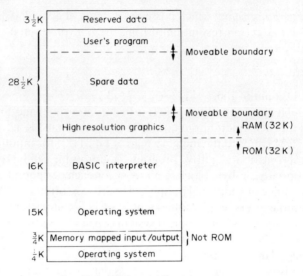

FIG. 11.5. BBC model B memory map.

Figure 11.5 shows a memory map for the BBC Model B micro-computer. The reader may like to compare this with the memory map for the Apple II (Fig. 11.2) and notice the similarities. The boundaries for the user's program and spare data area are not strictly defined for the BBC. Two blocks of memory mapped video are used by the Apple in comparison with only one by the BBC. The operating system is ROM-based in the BBC; it must be bootstrapped from floppy disk into RAM in the case of the Apple. Input/output is memory mapped in both cases.

In text-only mode the BBC microcomputer can display 24 rows of 40 characters in one mode; greater numbers of characters can be selected in different text modes. If the full screen is used for graphics, points and lines can be drawn on a matrix of 1279×1023. This gives much improved resolution over the Apple II. Additionally a flexible graphics "window" can be specified within a text display, e.g. the top left-hand corner can be the graphics area of the display.

A description of the BASIC commands and facilities which are available to the programmer are not presented here; the reader is referred to the *BBC Microcomputer User Guide*. The descriptions that follow emphasise the hardware interfacing facilities.

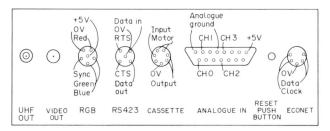

FIG. 11.6. BBC microcomputer rear panel.

Figure 11.6 shows the plug connections which are available on the rear panel of the BBC microcomputer. The signal drive to the television monitor is available on coaxial connections in UHF, video and RGB form. The RS 232-C serial channel is available on a DIN plug and is specified as a RS 423 signal; this is a minor variation of the standard RS 232-C. Primarily this channel (or serial port) is intended as a printer drive, but connection to a remote VDU or another computer could be made using the following three signals: data out, data in and 0 V. RTS (request to send) and CTS (clear to send) are available if required as handshaking signals between the two UARTs at each end of the link. If a serial printer is connected to this channel then only three connections are required to the printer plug, which is probably the D-type or Cannon plug (see section 3.3). These connections are:

BBC DIN plug	D-type printer plug
Data out	3
0 V	7
CTS	Variable (often 4; 20 for Qume printer)

If the machine is to use this serial port in place of the parallel printer connection (described later), then the user must enter a special command. Additionally a command must be typed in to select the required baud rate.

The audio cassette recorder interface is via another DIN plug. In addition to the input and output signal connections, a remote motor start signal is available. This is a relay-driven contact closure signal within the BBC microcomputer, and it can be connected at the recorder to switch the motor on automatically when programs are being transferred.

MI-G*

The "analogue in" socket is used for:

(a) Games paddles (1 analogue input each) ⎫ manual inputs for games,
(b) Joy-sticks (2 analogue inputs)   ⎭   etc.
(c) Transducers (and amplifiers), e.g. temperature, light intensity, weight.

The input voltage range is 0 to 1.8 V. The four analogue signals feed a 4-channel A/D converter within the machine.

The Econet connection is described later.

In addition to these rear panel connections, edge connectors on the main circuit board offer other interfacing facilities. In particular the MOS Technology 6522 PIO feeds one of its two ports to a parallel printer socket, and the other port to a spare user input/output socket. The circuit connections and address identities are shown in Fig. 11.7. MOS Technology term their 6522 PIO as a VIA (Versatile Interface Adaptor) and the device contains two ports, two counter/timer circuits and it handles an interrupt signal. For full information concerning the use of the device, e.g. initialising port directions and setting counters, the reader is referred to the manufacturer's data sheets. For example purposes here, the following BASIC program sets the user port B as an input port and then reads a byte from it:

```
10  REM Initialise port B as input
20  ?&FE62=0
30  REM Input from port B
40  SETTING=?&FE60
```

Alternatively a program can be entered in assembly language, e.g. to initialise port B as output in direction, and then to output a bit pattern of 1010 1010 to it:

```
500  LDA #&FF
510  STA &FE62
520  LDA #&AA
530  STA ?&FE60
```

Port A should not be initialised as an input port, since it is wired as an output port through drivers to the Centronics compatible parallel printer socket (26-way). This should be connected to the printer input socket, which is normally 36-way.

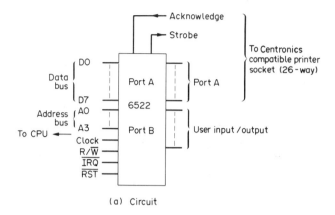

(a) Circuit

Address	Identity
FE60	Port B
FE61	Port A
FE62	Direction for port B
FE63	Direction for port A
FE64	TI low-order counter
FE65	TI high-order counter
FE66	TI low-order latches
FE67	T2 high-order latches
FE68	T2 low-order counter
FE69	T2 high-order counter
FE6A	Shift register
FE6B	Auxiliary control register
FE6C	Peripheral control register
FE6D	Interrupt flag register
FE6E	Interrupt enable register
FE6F	Port A (no handshake)

(b) 6522 address identities

Fig. 11.7. BBC PIO circuit.

One other extremely useful expansion socket is available on the BBC microcomputer, as shown in Fig. 11.8. The "1 MHz bus" connector on the main circuit board carries the 8 least significant address lines (for 256 memory mapped input/output addresses), the 8-bit data bus, address decoder output signals and appropriate control bus signals. Additional cards can be connected to this "bus"; cards are supplied by various manufacturers to provide additional serial and parallel channels, EPROM programmer, additional A/D and D/A, etc. One such add-on unit allows the computer to look at the usual range of BBC Ceefax and

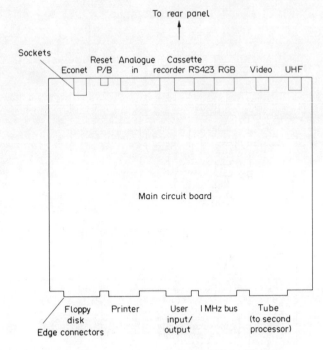

FIG. 11.8. Interfacing connectors on BBC microcomputer.

ITV Oracle pages. Additional programs (computer not television!) can be received via the aerial using the "telesoftware" system with this unit.

Another useful add-on unit which connects to the 1 MHz bus is the Prestel unit. This gives the normal British Telecom Prestel facilities, and includes the transmission of programs and data files between any two computers using the telephone network. A modem is included in this unit. Clearly the possible applications of this facility are wide-reaching and exciting.

The Econet connector allows up to 254 BBC computers to be connected together in a "local area network". Interconnections do not pass through the telephone network. A network of this type gives two attractive features:

(a) Expensive peripherals, e.g. floppy disk and printer, which are used

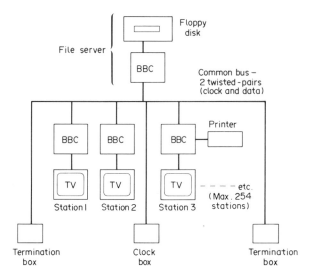

FIG. 11.9. Econet microcomputer network.

for only a small proportion of the time, can be shared by several computers.

(b) Messages and program/data files can be transmitted from one computer to another.

A common serial bus is used by all "stations"—see Fig. 11.9. A station is any BBC Model A or Model B computer. One master station may possess a floppy disk and is termed the "file server". One other may be connected to a printer.

Clearly only one data transfer operation can occur on the common bus at any time. If a transmitting station attempts to use the bus when it is already in use, a "collision" occurs and the station backs-off and waits until the bus is free.

One final connector on the BBC computer is termed the "Tube". This provides a high speed communications channel with a second processor. The second processor can be another computer, e.g. a 6502 board (with 64 K RAM), a Z80 board (with 64 K RAM and CP/M) or a National Semiconductors 16-bit 16032 board (with up to 16 Mbytes RAM).

BIBLIOGRAPHY

1. *BBC Micro*. James. Granada, 1983.
2. *Discovering BBC Micro Machine Code*. A. P. Stephenson. Granada, 1983.
3. *BBC Micro Revealed*. Rushton. Computer Workshop, 1983.

Appendix

ASCII CODE

Character	Hex.	Character	Hex.	Character	Hex.
NUL	00	SP	20	(a	40
SOH	01	!	21	A	41
STX	02	"	22	B	42
ETX	03	#	23	C	43
EOT	04	$	24	D	44
ENQ	05	%	25	E	45
ACK	06	&	26	F	46
BEL	07	'	27	G	47
BS	08	(	28	H	48
HT	09	)	29	I	49
LF	0A	*	2A	J	4A
VT	0B	+	2B	K	4B
FF	0C	,	2C	L	4C
CR	0D	-	2D	M	4D
S0	0E	.	2E	N	4E
S1	0F	/	2F	O	4F
DLE	10	0	30	P	50
DC1	11	1	31	Q	51
DC2	12	2	32	R	52
DC3	13	3	33	S	53
DC4	14	4	34	T	54
NAK	15	5	35	U	55
SYN	16	6	36	V	56
ETB	17	7	37	W	57
CAN	18	8	38	X	58
EM	19	9	39	Y	59
SUB	1A	:	3A	Z	5A
ESC	1B	;	3B	[	5B
FS	1C	<	3C	\	5C
GS	1D		3D	]	5D
RS	1E	>	3E	∧	5E
US	1F	?	3F		5F

Character	Hex.
	60
a	61
b	62
c	63
d	64
e	65
f	66
g	67
h	68
i	69
j	6A
k	6B
l	6C
m	6D

Character	Hex.
n	6E
o	6F
p	70
q	71
r	72
s	73
t	74
u	75
v	76
w	77
x	78
y	79
z	7A
{	7B

Character	Hex.
¦	7C
}	7D
~	7E
DEL	7F

Note

Characters hex. 00 to 1F are control characters.

Character hex. 7F is delete, or rub-out

Glossary

Accumulator. A special *CPU register* that receives the results of most *ALU* operations.

A/D converter. *Analogue* to *digital* converter.

Address bus. The *microcomputer bus* that carries the *memory* address of the *instruction* that is being fetched, or a *data* item that is being transferred between the *CPU* and memory or *input/output*.

Address decoder. A circuit that generates *chip select* signals for each *memory* or *input/output* *chip* within a *microcomputer*.

Addressing mode. A method of specifying the location of a *data* item which is accessed within an *instruction*.

ALU. Arithmetic and Logic Unit. The module within the *CPU* that performs arithmetic, e.g. add and subtract, and *logic*, e.g. *AND* and *OR* operations.

Analogue. A continuous signal that can take any value over its range.

AND. The *Boolean logic* function that generates logic 1 only if both comparison (or input) *bits* are also at logic 1.

ASCII. American Standard Code for Information Interchange. The code that is used to represent characters in *microcomputers*, printers and *VDUs*.

Assembler. A *program* that converts an *assembly language* program into *machine code*.

Assembly language. A programming *language* that is line-for-line convertible to *machine code*, but uses *mnemonics* and *labels* to assist the programmer.

Audio cassette recorder. A domestic tape recorder that is used to store *microcomputer programs*.

Backing store. A bulk storage device, e.g. *floppy disk* or *hard disk*, for *programs* and *data* files.

Base. The radix of a number system, e.g. the decimal system uses a base of 10 and the *binary* system uses a base of 2.

BASIC. Beginners All-purpose Symbolic Instruction Code. The most popular *high level language* that is used with *microcomputers*.

Baud rate. The speed of transmission of *serial data* expressed in *bits* per second.

Binary. A number system that uses the *base* of 2. The only symbols used in binary numbers are 0 and 1.

Bit. *Binary* digit. A bit has two states—0 and 1.

Boolean logic. A collection of *logic* functions named after George Boole. The Boolean logic functions *AND*, *OR* and *EXCLUSIVE OR* are applied by *software* on *binary* numbers in *microcomputers*.

Bootstrap. A *program* that reloads the main program into *memory* from *backing store* when the *computer* is switched on.

Bounce. Unwanted repeated operation of a mechanical contact.

Branch. As for *jump*.

Breakpoint. A stop that is inserted into a *program* to assist in the testing of a new or faulty program.

Buffer. A temporary storage *register*.

Bug. A *software* error.

Bus. A set of signal connections that have a common function. A *microcomputer* possesses an *address bus*, *data bus* and *control bus*.

Byte. Eight *bits*.

Call. An *instruction* that transfers *program* control to a *subroutine*.

Carry flag. A *bit* in a *CPU status register* which indicates that the result of an *ALU* operation has exceeded the number range of the ALU.

Central Processor Unit. See *CPU*.

Chip. A common name for an *integrated circuit*.

Chip select. A control signal that activates a *memory* or *input/output chip*.

CMOS. Complementary Metal Oxide Semiconductor. A family of *integrated circuits* that offers extremely high packing density and low power.

Common bus. A set of interfacing connections that allows *microcomputer* boards to be interconnected.

Compiler. A *program* that converts a *high level language* program into *machine code* before program run time and stores both versions on *backing store*.

Complement. Change a *bit* from 1 to 0 or from 0 to 1.

Computer. A programmable *data* processing system.

Control unit. The module within the *CPU* that examines and implements the current *instruction*.

Counter/timer. A programmable *input/output* circuit that can be used to generate timer *interrupt* pulses, generate time delays or count external pulses. Normally it is included in a *PIO chip*.

CPU. Central Processor Unit. The main *computer* module, which fetches and implements *program instructions*. Its main sub-modules are the *ALU* and *control unit*. In a *microcomputer* the CPU often forms a single *chip* and is called a *microprocessor*.

CRT. Cathode Ray Tube. A widely-used operator display device which is driven from the *computer*.

D/A converter. *Digital* to *analogue* converter.

Data. A general term that can describe numbers, characters or groups of *bits* suitable for processing within a *computer*.

Data bus. The *microcomputer bus* that carries *data* between *CPU* and *memory* or *input/output*.

Debugger. A *program* that is used to locate and eliminate errors (or *bugs*) in a test program.

Decimal. A number system that uses a *base* of 10.

Digit. Each symbol in a number system, e.g. a *binary* digit can be 0 or 1.

Digital. Possessing discrete states. *Computers* operate using *binary* digital signals, i.e. possessing only two states.

DIL. Dual In-Line. The standard *integrated circuit* package.

DMA. Direct Memory Access. *Data* transfer between *memory* and *input/output* without passing through the *CPU*.

Dot matrix. A method of constructing characters using an array of dots, e.g. printer and *CRT*.

Dynamic RAM. *RAM memory* that requires a regular refresh operation to prevent curruption of stored data.

EPROM. Erasable Programmable Read Only Memory. *ROM* that can be erased by exposure to ultra-violet light and then re-programmed.

EXCLUSIVE OR. The *Boolean logic* function that generates logic 1 only if both comparison (or input) *bits* are different.

Execute. To run a *program*. Alternatively the second part of the *fetch/execute* cycle which is implemented when the *CPU* obeys an *instruction*.

Fan-out. The maximum number of subsequent *gates* that the output signal connection from a gate can drive.

FET. Field Effect Transistor. The principal component in *MOS* and *CMOS* circuits.

Fetch. The first part in the *fetch/execute* cycle which is implemented when the *CPU* obeys an *instruction*.

Fetch/execute cycle. The basic cycle that is implemented by the *CPU* when it obeys an *instruction*. Firstly the instruction is fetched from *memory* and secondly it is examined by the *control unit* and executed.

Firmware. *Program* or *data* resident in *ROM*.

Flag. A *bit* that indicates a specific condition or event.

Floppy disk. A *backing store* medium that employs flexible magnetic disks.

Flowchart. The diagrammatic representation of the operation of a *program*.

Gate. A *digital* circuit with more than one input, but only one output. Gates can perform *Boolean logic* functions.

Hard disk. A backing store medium that employs a non-removable hard disk. A hard disk is faster, more expensive and possesses larger storage capacity than a *floppy disk*. It is often called a "Winchester".

Hardware. The physical equipment in a *computer*.

Hexadecimal. A number system that uses a *base* of 16. Its particular use is to represent long *binary* numbers, which are used in *microcomputers*, in a shorter form.

High level language. A programming *language* that is similar to spoken language. A high level language program must be converted into *machine code* before it is run in a *computer*.

IC. *Integrated circuit.*

In-circuit emulator. A combined *hardware* and *software* system that is used in a *MDS* to test a new *microprocessor*-based product.

Initialise. To set an *input/output chip*, e.g. a *PIO*, *UART* or *counter/timer*, to one of its programmable states.

Input/output. The *hardware* within a *computer* that connects the computer to external *peripherals* and devices.

Input port. A circuit that passes external *digital* signals (normally 8) into a *microcomputer*.

Instruction. A single operation performed by a *computer*. A *low level language program* consists of a list of instructions.

Integrated circuit. A circuit package that contains several components built into the same semiconductor wafer.

Interface. To interconnect a *computer* to external devices and circuits.

Interrupt. An external signal that suspends a *program* operating within a *computer* and causes entry into a special interrupt program. The latter is normally named an *interrupt service routine*.

Interrupt service routine. A *program* that is entered following an *interrupt*.

Jump. An *instruction* that sends *program* control to a specified *memory* location.

K. A symbol that represents *decimal* 1024.

Kansas Standard. A signal specification for *data* storage on *audio cassette recorders*.

Label. A name given to a *memory* location in an *assembly language program*.

Language. A prescribed set of characters and symbols which is used to convey a *program* to a *computer*. A programming language can be a *high level language* or a *low level language*.

Latch. A circuit that staticises *bits*.

LCD. Liquid Crystal Display. A very low-powered numeric display that operates on the principle of reflecting incident light.

LED. Light Emitting Diode. A diode that emits light when current passes through it. A LED is commonly applied with *microcomputers* to indicate a condition or event, e.g. machine on/off, and in the structure of *segment displays*.

Logic. The application of a range of circuit building blocks to perform switching and control functions.

Logic analyser. An item of test equipment that can display the state of several *logic* levels.

Logic level. The voltage value that is used to indicate *logic* 0 or 1. Normally +5 V = logic 1, and 0 V = logic 0.

Loop. A section of *program* that is executed more than once.

Low level language. A *computer* programming *language* that specifies each operation that the *CPU* is to perform. There are two classifications of low level language: *assembly language* and *machine code*.

LSI. Large Scale Integration. A measure of the packing density of an *integrated circuit* (greater than 100 *gates* per *chip*). See *SSI*, *MSI* and *VLSI*.

M. A symbol that represents a million. See also *K*.

Machine code. A *program* expressed in *binary* form, i.e. in the way in which it is executed within the *CPU*.

Main memory. Fast *memory* which holds the *program* currently being executed. Main memory can be *ROM*, *RAM* or a mixture of the two.

Matrix printer. A printer that constructs characters using a *dot matrix*.

MDS. Microprocessor Development System. A *computer* that is used to develop *software* for prototype *microcomputer* applications.

Memory. Any circuit or *peripheral* that staticises *data*. Normally the term is used in place of *main memory*.

Memory mapped input/output. *Input/output* devices that are treated by *hardware* and *software* as *memory* devices.

Microcomputer. A complete *computer* on a handful of *integrated circuits* (or even a single integrated circuit). *VLSI* components are used for *CPU*, *memory* and *input/output*.

Microprocessor. A *CPU* constructed on a single *VLSI integrated circuit*.

Mnemonic. A group of letters that is used to represent the function of an *instruction* expressed in *assembly language* form.

Monitor. The main *program* in many *microcomputers*.

MOS. Metal Oxide Semiconductor. A family of *integrated circuits* that offers high packing density. MOS technology is used to construct *microprocessors*, *ROM*, *RAM* and many *input/output* devices.

MSI. Medium Scale Integration. A measure of the packing density of an *integrated circuit* (greater than 10 *gates* per *chip*). See *SSI*, *LSI* and *VLSI*.

Multiplexing. The technique of passing more than one signal along a single conductor.

NAND. The *Boolean logic NOT AND* function.

Nesting. A *program loop* within another loop. A *subroutine* within another subroutine. An *interrupt service routine* within another interrupt service routine.

NOR. The *Boolean logic NOT OR* function.

NOT. The *Boolean logic* function that inverts a logic level or a *bit*.

Object code. The name given to a *machine code* version of a *program*. The term is used to distinguish this version from the *assembly language* version (called the "source program").

Octal. A number system that uses a *base* of 8.

Opcode. The part of a *machine code instruction* that specifies the function of the instruction, e.g. add, *shift*, *jump*.

Operand. The part of a *machine code instruction* that specifies the *data* value or its *memory* address.

Operating system. The main *program* in a disk-based *microcomputer*.

OR. The *Boolean logic* function that generates logic 1 if either of the comparison (or input) *bits* is set to logic 1.

Output port. A circuit that passes *digital* signals (normally a group of 8) outside a *microcomputer*.

Parity. The number, expressed as odd or even, of 1s in a *data* value.

PCB. Printed Circuit Board. A conventional circuit board with etched copper track interconnection between components.

Peripheral. An item of equipment that is external to a *computer*, e.g. printer, *VDU*, *floppy disk*.

PIO. Parallel Input/Output. A programmable multi-*port input/output* chip.

PLC. Programmable Logic Controller. An industrial sequence control system—frequently *microcomputer*-based.

Poll. To regularly check the status of an external signal or device by *software*.

Port. An input or output channel between a *microcomputer* and external equipment. Normally a port is 8-*bits* wide.

Program. A set of processing steps that a *computer* is required to perform.

Program counter. A *CPU register* that holds the address in *memory* of the next *instruction* to be obeyed.

PROM. Programmable Read Only Memory. *ROM* that is programmed after the *chip* is manufactured. Once programmed it cannot be altered.

RAM. Random Access Memory. RAM is semiconductor read/write *memory*. It is misnamed because *ROM* is also random access.

Read. To transfer *data* from *memory* to the *CPU*.

Refresh. To re-instate *data* stored in *dynamic RAM* or displayed on a *CRT* or *segment display*.

Register. A storage device for several *bits*. A *microprocessor* contains several work registers, which can be used for temporary storage of *data* within a *program*.

Return. An *instruction* that returns *program* control to a main program from a *subroutine* or an *interrupt service routine*.

ROM. Read Only Memory. ROM is semiconductor *memory* which can only be read. There are three common classifications of ROM: ROM, *PROM* and *EPROM*.

RS 232-C. The internationally-recognised specification for *serial data* transfer between *computers* and serial-drive *peripherals*.

SBC. Single Board Computer. A complete *microcomputer* circuit on a single board.

S-100 bus. The most widely used *common bus* applied in multi-board *microcomputer* construction.

Segment display. A display that constructs numbers and letters by a network of segments. *Microcomputers* commonly use 7-segment displays for representing numbers.

Semiconductor memory. *ROM* and *RAM*.

Serial. The transfer of *data* items by setting one *bit* at a time on a single conductor.

Shift. Transfer of *data* to the left or right.

Software. *Computer programs* and *data* files.

Source program. The name given to the *assembly language* version of a *program*.

SSI. Small Scale Integration. A measure of the packing density of an *integrated circuit* (less than 10 *gates* per *chip*). See *MSI*, *LSI* and *VLSI*.

Stack. A reserved area of *memory* (*RAM*) that is used in many *microprocessors* to store the return address in *subroutines* and *interrupt service routines*.

Status register. A collection of *flag bits* in a *microprocessor* that indicates the state of the *ALU*.

Subroutine. A section of *program* that is separated from the main program, but can be called several times from the main program.

Three-state (or **Tri-state**). A circuit in which its outputs can be set into one of three states—*logic* 0, logic 1 or "floating" (high impedance state, i.e. electrically disconnected).

TTL. Transistor Transistor Logic. A family of *integrated circuits* that preceded *MOS* and *CMOS*, but still offers the advantage of much faster operating speed. However, packing density is low in TTL and power consumption is much higher than for MOS and CMOS. Typically a full *microcomputer* circuit includes MOS *CPU*, *ROM* and *RAM*, but also TTL *gates* and *buffers*.

TTY. Teletype. A name sometimes used for a printer.

Two's complement. A *binary* numbering system used to represent both positive and negative numbers.

UART. Universal Asynchronous Receiver Transmitter. An *input/output chip* that handles *serial data* transfer, e.g. to *VDU*, printer or other *computer*.

Unipolar. A transistor that uses only one charge carrier. A more familiar name is *FET*.

VDU. Visual Display Unit. An operator device that includes a *CRT* for display purposes and a keyboard for manual entry.

Vector. A fixed *memory* location that contains the start address of an *interrupt service routine*.

Volatile memory. *Memory* that loses its stored *bit* pattern when power is removed.

VLSI. Very Large Scale Integration. A measure of the packing density of an *integrated circuit* (more than 1000 *gates* per chip). See *MSI*, *LSI* and *SSI*.

Winchester. Another name for a *hard disk*.

Word. A unit of *data* in a *microcomputer*. The word length is the same as the *bit* length of the *microprocessor*, i.e. normally either 8 bits or 16 bits.

Write. To transfer *data* from *CPU* to *memory*.

Write protect. To set a *backing store* device to read-only to protect against over-writing.

SUBJECT INDEX